Turkmenistan

Adventures on the Silk Road

Simon Proudman

FARFLUNGPLACES

Turkmenistan

Adventures on the Silk Road

© Simon Proudman.

1st Edition. 2014. All rights reserved.

ISBN 978-1500271138

E-mail: info@farflungplaces.net

Keep in Touch - Follow Far Flung Places on Social Media

Blog: www.farflungplaces.net/

Twitter: www.twitter.com/farflungplaces

Facebook: www.facebook.com/farflungplaces.net

Pinterest: www.pinterest.com/farflungplaces/

StumbleUpon:
www.stumbleupon.com/stumbler/Farflungplaces

Thanks to Joyce for her editing, Alison for her suggestions, Lea for all of the above and so much more, my father for sparking my interest in travel, and to all those who read and contribute to my blog.

Map of Turkmenistan

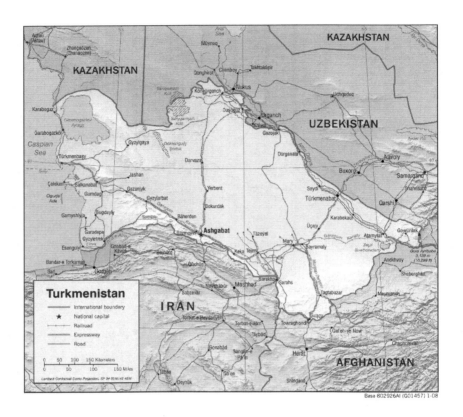

Table of Contents

Introduction

Congratulations, if you are going to Turkmenistan and already have a visa you are a rarity. **Only 6500 tourist visas were issued in 2012.** Tourism is not viewed as important by the government, and with the vast sums being earned in oil and gas, this view will probably not change for while.

If you are not planning to go to Turkmenistan quite yet, this Far Flung Places guide is guaranteed to pique your interest and encourage you to visit one of the most unusual and fascinating countries in the world.

Maybe you enjoy being an armchair traveller. This book is for you to sit back and imagine yourself travelling through this amazing and interesting country.

Travel can be difficult to arrange, and occasionally frustrating, but it is an unforgettable experience with beautiful and rarely visited ancient ruins from the Silk Road, such as Merv and Gurganj, the unique experience of the collapsed gas field, the Gates Of Hell, a totalitarian regime, with a reputation just behind North Korea for Press Freedom (see http://www.freedomhouse.org/article/10-worst-countries-journalists) and being one of the last two Stalinist states remaining, yes, North Korea is the other one.

Both countries focus on Personality Cults for their leaders, but Turkmenistan goes considerably further, with its previous leader, Saparmurat Niyazov, (also known as Turkmenbashy, a self given name meaning Leader of Turkmen) not only placing statues of himself in every open space, outside schools, hospitals and universities, but creating his own 'Bible', the Rukhana, and renaming the months and days of the week after his relatives and Turkmen heroes.

Why stop there? He did not. He renamed bread after his mother, and banned beards, long hair, gold caps on teeth (a notable failure as you will see if you wander around any Bazaar in Turkmenistan) and lip-synching. He must have been as traumatised as many of the youth of Europe were when he discovered Milli Vanilli lip-synched their way to a Grammy in the Eighties.

He banned dogs, because of their smell, circuses, because they were 'un-Turkmen' and even female newsreaders wearing makeup, as they were beautiful already being Turkmen women.

Just after announcing he would remain leader for life, President Niyazov died. His physician, Gurbanguly Berdimuhamedow took over. This led to some wild speculation, told to me by several Turkmen people, that he may have had a hand in this.

Berdimuhamedow did not immediately establish his own cult of personality, nor destroy his predecessors, leading many to think that maybe he would be more progressive. However the signs are not promising: photographs and pictures of him are appearing all over the country, he has published his own musings on life (not quite the Rukhana, yet), has adopted the title of Arakadag (The Patron), and much of the National Museum (see the Ashgabat chapter) is devoted to him in often hilarious poses.

I have a feeling that the first gold statue cannot be that far away.

Turkmenistan: The Basics

Statue of a Turkmen warrior at the Independence Monument Park in Ashgabat.

Where is Turkmenistan?

Turkmenistan is located in the southernmost part of Central Asia, east of the Caspian Sea.

Our Top 10 things to do in Turkmenistan

❖ Warm yourself on a cold desert night next to the 'Gate to Hell' in Derweze.

❖ Visit the mud brick fortress of the Great Gyzgala in Merv.

❖ Head to a restaurant for a fresh meal of Plov with Non bread.

❖ Walk around the shining white marble buildings, and gold statues in downtown Ashgabat.

❖ Try and fit the huge Kutlug Timur Minaret in Gurganj into your camera viewfinder.

❖ Shop for carpets at the Altyn Asyr market outside Ashgabat.

❖ Wander around the fruit, music and wedding stalls in the Central Bazaar in Mary.

❖ Climb the ancient walls of Erk Kala in Merv and imagine life in one of Alexander the Greats favourite cities.

❖ Eat samosas on the banks of the River Margush in Mary.

❖ Visit the National Museum in Ashgabat and see the photographic galleries devoted to the current President.

Itineraries

You can rush through Turkmenistan on a 3-day transit visa trying to fly everywhere but you will only get a very brief glimpse of the country and will miss some key sites. The 'must-see' spots for any tour should include Merv, Ashgabat and Gurganj, and if you have the time, the burning gas crater at Derweze.

I would recommend at least two days to explore Ashgabat and its surrounding area, including a weekend day if possible to see the Altyn Asyr market. Then take a trip to Mary either by train, if you book far enough in advance, or by plane. Spend two days here to fully take in the sites of the ancient city of Merv. Then travel to Dashoguz to visit Gurganj for a day. To fit in an overnight trip to the Derweze (the gas crater is best seen at night, and the stars in the desert sky are unforgettable) you generally have to start from Ashgabat. The trip to Derweze can also be done as part of a road trip onto Dashoguz and Gurganj.

This itinerary can be completed in a rushed week, but I would recommend **spending ten days** or more in this fascinating country.

While you are in Central Asia you can combine a visit to Turkmenistan with travelling to the architectural treasures of Uzbekistan. Two of its major ancient cities, Khiva and Bukhara were once part of Turkmenistan and are located close to the border. Samarkand, further north, is an unforgettable city with the Registan and the remains of Afrosiab.

Both Iran and Kazakhstan are easily visited from Turkmenistan, and should Afghanistan become safe to travel in again it hosts many important archaeological sites forming part of the great Silk Road link to Merv.

The Amu Daryu River, the Oxus River of antiquity, forms the border between Uzbekistan and Turkmenistan

A Short History of Turkmenistan

Early History

Neolithic remains of human habitation have been found near Nissa, just outside of modern Ashgabat. The desert oasis there provided water for agriculture and settlement. Small villages began to grow on the coast, and near rivers, but these were mostly nomadic. Turkmenistan became a place to invade and occupy, firstly by the Persians, and then by Alexander the Great in 330 BC on his way towards conquering Asia.

Turkmenistan was occupied by the Persians and Scythians (from the North), forming the Parthian empire. It was continually fought over by Persians, Huns and Turks, until Genghis Khan and the Mongols conquered the land in the 13th century. They controlled the area for the next two centuries until they were overthrown in the late 15th century by invading Uzbeks.

Turkmenistan rarely knew peace, it became the site of a power struggle between Uzbeks, Persians and the Khans, two great leaders who established the city-states of Bukhara and Khiva (now, confusingly thanks to the Russians redrawing country borders, in Uzbekistan).

Russia began sending exploratory military expeditions into Turkmenistan in the second half of the 19th century, defeating and annexing the khanates of Bukhara and Khiva in 1868. The people of western Turkmenistan, who were seeking independence from the Khans, willingly joined the Russian Empire. In eastern and southern Turkmenistan the inhabitants fiercely resisted the Russians.

In 1879, at Geok-Tepe near Ashgabat, Turkmen fought and stopped a large Russian force. But two years later they were defeated and by 1895, all of Turkmenistan was controlled by Russia.

Last Century

During the Russian revolution of 1917 anti Bolshevik forces retained Ashgabat and established the independent state of Transcapia, with help from a small British force, before the Soviets reclaimed all of Turkmenistan in 1920, and it was proclaimed part of the newly formed U.S.S.R in 1925.

Independence

With the collapse of the Soviet Union, Turkmenistan became independent on October 27th 1991. The former head of the Communist party during Soviet times, Niyazov, was elected president in a unanimous uncontested vote. He developed a totalitarian cult of personality, banned opposition parties and in 1999 amended the country's constitution to allow himself to be president for life.

Turkmenistan soldiers on guard outside the Independence Monument in Ashgabat.

This Century

In 2006 Niyazov died unexpectedly of heart disease, with no deputy or other clear alternative to take over. Breaking the country's constitution, the Health Minister, and Niyazov's personal Doctor, Berdimuhamedow, became acting president.

The country's first free contested elections were held in February 2007, and, amid much criticism that they were marred by fraud, Berdimuhamedow was declared the winner and was formally inaugurated as Turkmenistan's second president.

THE PRESIDENT FOR A LIFE OF
INDEPENDENT AND NEUTRAL TURKMENISTAN
SAPARMYRAT TURKMENBASHY THE GREAT

Niyazov, President for Life (Image from the Rukhana, 2006).

The Silk Road

The Silk Road was one of the greatest trade routes ever developed. Linking China and the Roman Empire, the two strongest civilizations in the world two thousand years ago, it crossed mountains, deserts, and inland seas. The common perception of it is as one long road connecting X'ian to Rome, but in reality it was a linked network of overland routes connecting major cities.

Extensive camel trains often exceeding 1000 animals moved from city to city, travelling at night across deserts to avoid the heat, and joining with other traders for safety against the opportunistic robbers and bandits who hid in the mountains.

Central Asia was in the middle of the Silk Road with key routes crossing Uzbekistan and Turkmenistan. The most traveled route passed through Kashgar to Samarkand, Bukhara and Merv. In Merv the Silk Road split. One branch went via Gurganj and then onto Eastern Europe and Russia. Another branch went via Balkh and into the lands of modern Afghanistan to India. The third branch went to Persia, then Constantinople, and onto ports on the Mediterranean Sea. Here the goods were loaded on ships and delivered to Europe.

Cities on the route flourished with the influx of trade and money. Caravanserais were built along the road. These were rest places located approximately 25km apart, which was the most the camel trains and horses could travel in a day. The more successful of these Caravanserais grew into cities, offering more than just accommodation and food. They developed specialties in producing goods sought by the traders, growing livestock to provide replacement animals, and establishing markets where goods could be exchanged.

The trade was more than just silk, a term coined by a late-19th-century German geographer, Ferdinand von Richthofen (uncle of the famed first world war fighter pilot, the Red Baron). Silk provided an impetus for the trade from China, as Romans discovered and demanded the fine fabric for their togas in the first century AD. The Romans were besotted with the imported luxury item, naming China 'Seres', or the country of silk. Such was the demand for silk, it resulted in a substantial financial drain on the economy by diverting resources to its importation. This was a contributory factor to the decline of the Roman Empire.

Many more goods were traded; gunpowder, paper, wheelbarrows, tea, iron, nickel and furs made their way from China, while Europe sent amber, glass, ceramics, textiles, gold and wine. The trade was more than two way, with China importing cotton and Saffron from India, horses from Uzbekistan, ostriches from Persia, and melons from Turkmenistan, while Europe introduced pistachios, muslin and indigo from India and Asia.

A fortress connected to the city wall at the Silk Road city of Merv

Ideas, languages and culture were also spread, as Christianity and Buddhism was carried from place to place, along with art and philosophies. The road was also responsible for the transportation of death and disease, being responsible for introduction of the Black Death to Crimea in the fourteenth century.

The concept of travel, and the means to do it were embodied in the growth of the trading route. Travelers would pay to be passengers to go from city to city riding camels, or horses. The first passport was introduced on the route to ease the passage of travelers passing through the Mongol empire.

The decline of the Silk Road began when trade by sea began to be both cheaper and faster in the fifteenth century. In a neat reversal of current economic trends, the unique products of China; silk, gunpowder and paper, were copied, and produced more cheaply in Europe, reducing the need for large amounts of imports. With China also retreating to focus inward and stay behind the Great Wall under the rule of Ming, the cities on the Silk Road began to whither and die.

In Turkmenistan the Silk Road provided the impetus for Merv in particular to flourish, while Amul, Gurganj and Nissa also grew due to the caravan trains that passed through. Merv grew to become the largest city in the world due to its position at the crossroads to the network of trade routes. The decline of the Silk Road mirrors the decline of the Turkmenistan ancient cities, with Merv in particular marooned in the desert, and at the mercy of foreign armies.

Geography

Turkmenistan is the most southern most part of the former Soviet Union, and is now aligned as a member state of the Commonwealth of Independent States (CIS), the bloc of Russian friendly states created post 1991.

The size of the country is 488,100 square km (188,500 square miles), and in comparison is just larger than the US state of California.

In the north it borders Kazakhstan, in the northeast Uzbekistan, in the east Afghanistan, and in the south Iran. It has a 1768 km border with the Caspian Sea, and through the Volga Don canal gives the country trade route access to the Black Sea.

Most of the country, over 80%, comprises of the Kara Kum desert. In the south and southwest are the Kopet Dag and Paropamisus mountain ranges.

With so much of the country desert, the main rivers have been extremely important in the development of the country. The largest is the Amy Darya (the Oxus of antiquity) stretching 2,540 km across Turkmenistan, and then into Uzbekistan and Tajikistan. Mass irrigation projects in Soviet times, mainly for the production of cotton, have dramatically reduced the flow of the river and have contributed to the drying up of the Aral Sea and the environmental devastation mostly affecting Uzbekistan.

Other major rivers include the Tejen, Murghab and the Atrek.

Turkmenistan is rich in natural resources with huge deposits of gas and oil. A massive pipeline is currently being constructed to provide liquefied natural gas (LNG) to China. Other resources include potash, rare earth metals and gold.

It has a subtropical arid desert climate, since the country lacks contact with an ocean. Summers are long, hot and dry, and precipitation is only slight and occurs in the first few months at the beginning of the year.

Population

The last census in 2001 recorded the population of Turkmenistan amounting to 4,603,200 people. Due to the country being predominantly desert the average population density is a low 9.43 person per square metre.

A variety of nationalities live in Turkmenistan. At 72% the largest group is Turkmen, but they are joined by large communities of Russians (9.5%), Uzbeks (9%) and Kazakhs (2.5%). There are also small minorities of Ukrainian, Kurds, Tatars, Armenians and Pashtun ethnic groups.

The number of Russians, which once made up over 20% of the population has continued to decline since the break up of the Soviet Union. The decision in 2003 to outlaw dual citizenship, forcing the still sizeable Russian population to choose whether to have a Turkmen or Russian passport, added to the exodus. The Russian language is still taught in schools and over 50% of the population are Russian speakers, although Turkmen has been the official language since 1992.

Sunni Muslims make up 89% of the population, with 10% being Eastern Orthodox Christians.

There are many Turkmen in surrounding states, with over 1 million living in Iran, and 650,000 in Afghanistan., and smaller numbers in Pakistan and Uzbekistan.

Economy

In Soviet times Turkmenistan was recognised as being a source of oil and natural gas, but much of its reserves were not discovered until after independence in 1991, which gave the new President a nice windfall and huge amounts of money to play with. Today Turkmenistan is recognised as having the world's fourth largest reserves of natural gas, with regular discoveries of more gas in the Kara Kum desert. This has coincided with large increases in the price of these resources, helping power the annual GDP rate into double figures for most of the last ten years.

The differences between the oil and gas rich Turkmenistan and the less resource rich Uzbekistan, where I had arrived from, were many. Even my taxi driver in Ashgabat had an iPhone, while old Nokia phones were prevalent in Tashkent.

Exports and growth are now linked totally to one commodity, natural gas, leaving the traditional Soviet mainstay of cotton to dwindle in comparison. The rivers of money flowing into the economy have helped support the leaders' grand visions for rivaling Dubai, pouring money into huge marble clad buildings, rebuilding the heart of Ashgabat so that it resembles the sterility and shiny surface of a major hospital.

The people have benefited from many handouts, although unemployment is high and boredom and dissatisfaction can be seen in a younger generation which has mainly two choices; to try and gain a highly sought after government job, or to chase the few opportunities in the natural gas industry.

Wandering around Ashgabat at night you will see an extravagant show of electricity. All the buildings have the lights on, with floodlights used to reflect off the marble. It would be every child's dream, a country where no parent will tell them to switch off the bedroom light they left on.

Electricity is free to all, as is water. The city blazes night and day, no one hits the off switch. As of January 2014, the President announced that gas meters would be installed in each house, so it is possible that there is the intention to start charging for this resource. Petrol was free with each driver getting a monthly quota of 120 litres, however this was removed in July 30th 2014, and drivers will now pay the equivalent of 22 cents per litre.

It will be interesting to see what happens if this policy changes for electricity, but for now even the poorest Turkmen people I met live with air conditioning pumping out day and night. Spending a little time in a rural area I was surprised that the farmers placed heaters in animal pens, to keep their cows and pigs warm in winter. Even the cattle benefit from the resources boom.

The closed Ashgabat Circus building at night.

Needless to say 'Earth Hour' or the idea of Green politics doesn't do well here. In fact politics in general tend to suffer when the President prefers to rule for life.

Note: All references to $ in this guide refer to the US dollar. Like it or not, it is the most accepted currency in the region. The Turkmen New Manat is referred to as TM$.

Visa Requirements

Tourism is not considered important by the government, and with the vast sums being earned in oil and gas, this view will probably not change.

It can be a hard and expensive country to visit. The visa application process takes a while, and then there still can be problems entering the country. And to further discourage tourists, the Turkmenistan government now demands you have, and pay for, a guide with you at all times if you want to spend more than a few days in the country. Luckily the definition of a guide is a bit loose, and if you have a driver travelling with you, even if he does not speak a word of English, that is counted as a guide. But this still can add up to approximately $US50 or more per day in costs.

All visas require forms to be obtained from your nearest Turkmenistan consulate. Currently trying to obtain the forms from the consulate website gives you an unavailable '404 Unknown Page Error', so you need to contact the consulate directly.

Consulates are located in the US, UK, France, Germany and select other countries outside of Eastern Europe, but not in Australia or New Zealand, see full list in Appendix 1.

Completed forms and passport, two passport photographs and the appropriate fees, which differ widely from country to country, will then need to be sent to the consulate. The whole process can take up to six weeks. It is a bit of a hassle, but do not be put off, it is worth it!

There are there three main visa types:

Transit Visa

Valid for three days only, but increasingly hard to obtain. In the past they were available for 5 days or more, but the government has cracked down on these from most embassies, suggesting you require a tourist visa if you need more time. They are valid between two land border crossings only, for example between Iran and Uzbekistan. You cannot fly out of Ashgabat on a transit visa, nor can you double back. For example, you cannot arrive from, and then return to, Uzbekistan. All in all, very restrictive and you will have to race across the country using public transport.

Tourist Visa

You can stay up to three weeks, and have freedom to roam in Turkmenistan. You have to nominate where you are going to travel, and some areas will still not be approved (anywhere near the Afghanistan border in particular). So you need to have planned your itinerary before you apply.

You will need to collect a guide at you entry point, and will say goodbye at the exit point, however if you book a tour through a travel company you will be likely to get a local guide in each city (avoiding hotel costs for the guide as they stay in their own homes) and have a driver, if you are travelling by car, nominated as the guide.

If you want to travel independently you will have to pay for the guides' accommodation. This is half the cost, or less, of the price charged to a foreign tourist, but still the costs do mount up.

Tourist visas are arranged through travel agents, and they will apply for the letter of introduction (LOI), which will list all the places and regions you are allowed to visit. They also arrange tours, either as part of a group or on your own.

The latest list of Travel Agents authorised to process LOIs with the Turkmenistan government are listed in Appendix II. I arranged mine extremely swiftly and easily in Uzbekistan through Advantours in Tashkent (details in Appendix II).

The Turkmenistan government (the State Service for the Registration of Foreign Nationals) will have to approve the LOI, a process that can take up to two weeks, and even then you can be rejected for no apparent reason. Two German tourists I met in Merv had to apply three times before being accepted. Once approved, you will receive an email of the LOI that you can send or take it to your local Turkmenistan consulate for

One of the many gold statues erected by Niyazov in Ashgabat.

a visa to be issued. The issuing of a visa is a formality; it is the LOI which is the most important document. If you are coming from a country that does not have a Turkmenistan consulate such as Australia, Singapore or New Zealand, you will be able to pick up a visa upon arrival. If possible get the name of the first guide you will meet at your entry point (see the Land Crossings section of this guide to understand the problems that may occur).

Once you have met your guide, he will hand over a folder of documents to the Immigration official, including three copies of a green Entry Travel Pass, which requires stamping. You will pay an extra US$10 for the Pass, plus US$2 for processing. The official will keep one, you get to keep one, and the last one is surrendered on your exit location, which is written on it. Do not lose these, as officials will be happy to levy all sorts of fines on you. It is possible to change your route, and length of stay in the country, but not guaranteed. In any case you need to do this via your travel agent, and will have to pay several fees, and wait for approval.

Business Visa

If you are lucky enough to be invited to work in Turkmenistan by a local business, you will get a local Letter of Introduction alongside a description of the work you will be doing. No need for a guide and a lot more freedom than a Tourist or Transit Visa, but obviously a little harder to get.

Festivals and Holidays

Apart from October, when visas are hard to come by (see the 'When to go' section) to be in Turkmenistan during a holiday can be a great time to visit. Parties and barbeques, with huge amounts of meat on the grill, are held in residential areas, and being foreign you will be invariably invited to join in the fun and celebrations.

Turkmenistan observes twelve public holidays:

- 1 January - New Year

- 12 January - Memorial Day

- 18 February - Turkmenbashi Birthday

- 19 February - National Flag Day

- 8 March - International Women's Day

- 20 March - Novruz-Bayram (Turkmen New Year)

- 9 May - Victory Day

- 18 May - Constitution Day

- 21 June - Day of election of First President

- 6 October- Day of Remembrance of the victims of the earthquake in 1948

- 28 October - Independence Day

- 12 December - Neutrality Day

The major Islamic holidays of Eid al-Adha and Ramadan are also observed. Since both these dates are calculated according to the lunar Islamic calendar, the dates of these celebrations vary and are announced annually by the Turkmenistan government.

When to go

Turkmenistan is hot. Very hot, due to its location, and with over 80% of it being the Karkum desert, it is the hottest country in Central Asia.

The Worst time to visit

The worst time to go is July to September, when temperatures can exceed 50°C. If you do travel then, take lots of water, and avoid going out in the heat of the day (11AM to 3PM). Consider that desert sites like Merv are almost impossible to visit at the peak of summer.

The northern hemisphere winter makes desert temperatures fall below freezing at night from late December to early March.

Best time to visit

The coolest and most pleasant times to visit are from March to early June and November to December.

Avoid

October, around Independence Day, is to be avoided, not because of the weather, which is in fact perfect for travelling, but because the Turkmenistan government has a great reluctance to issue tourist visas for this time, and there is a high chance your application will be rejected.

Time

Turkmenistan used to straddle several of the USSR's time zones, but now runs five hours ahead of GMT across the whole country. There is no daylight savings time, unlike Iran and Kazakhstan.

How to get there

By Air:

Turkmenistan Airways fly direct to Ashgabat from Abu-Dhabi, Alma-Ata, Amritsar, Bangkok, Birmingham, Delhi, Dubai, Frankfurt, Kiev, London, Minsk, Moscow, Beijing, Istanbul, Riga, Paris and St Petersburg.

The airline has modern aircraft and a good safety record currently. There is a slightly disturbing painting of the President Gurbanguly Berdimuhamedow (henceforth known as the 'Leader' for short) with a somewhat forced smile for the front rows to stare at for entertainment instead of the more customary video screens.

Arriving at Ashgabat, Turkmenbashy airport is a great introduction to the country. The gates for disembarkation are marble and stone, and look stunning and unreal. But, as they are not the movable aero bridge you have come to expect at airports they cannot actually be used by the aircraft for fear of damaging the planes. You disembark by the stairs. As with the other 'stans expect long waits at passport control, customs and luggage collection.

A rather special feature of this airport was that the first President, Saparmurat Niyazov, altered the actual design plans himself in order to produce a world famous monument to Turkmenistan's modernity. This resulted in the control tower being built in the centre of the airport, with the ornate and large terminal buildings surrounding it, and, rather uniquely for an airport, blocking the view of air traffic controllers as they attempt to guide pilots.

By Sea

From Azerbaijan is possible, but fraught with difficulties, as you have to use cargo ships and have plenty of time to spare waiting around, and plenty of time on your visa (which might expire).

By Land Crossing

You can cross from Iran, Kazakhstan and Uzbekistan. Land border crossings, are both fun and frustrating. You need to have plenty of time, much patience and a good book to read. I used two crossings, Farab (Bukhara in Uzbekistan to Turkmenabad) and the Khojeli crossing (Konye-Urgench to Nukus in Uzbekistan).

How difficult can it be? Travelling through Turkmenistan Land Crossings

The Farab Crossing - I took a taxi from Bukhara for $10 for an hour journey to a pretty desolate place with a few farms on a rutted road that seemed to go nowhere, until the barbed wire and border gates appear. The Uzbek side of the border is run down with fans that do not work in summer and the only air conditioning being in the two passport control booths, which not surprisingly, are full of officials.

I stood with dozens of Uzbek and Turkmen families carrying huge bags and resigned to a long wait in sweltering conditions. There are no chairs available. Being a foreigner can sometimes bring some advantages: one of the senior Uzbek officials who had been hiding out in the passport booth saw me, and dragged me to the front of the queue and through the x ray scanners and customs inspectors. The rest of the queue did not seem angry or surprised, and I was thankful to be actually getting closer to crossing into Turkmenistan.

The actual formalities were completed swiftly and I walked out into No Mans land, a 1 KM cracked road packed with trucks waiting to pass into each country. There was supposed to be a bus to carry you, charging $1, or TM$1, or UZ1000. It was not running, so I dragged my bag bouncing down the road for 30 minutes chatting to patient truck drivers who seemed to have taken up residency, with small tents, camping chairs and gas cookers, sharing their food and drink with a rare passer by.

The Turkmenistan border control was shiny, with expensive marble (oh how the Turkmenistan government loves marble, they are the biggest

A Turkmen Driver waits patiently by his truck in no mans land between Uzbekistan and Turkmenistan.

importer of Italian marble in the world) and gold trimmings. It resembled more of an extravagant and gaudy bathroom than a government building.

There were two checks of my passport and visa, first of all in a small room as I entered the building where the soldier who checked me was jovial and extremely happy to see an Australian. He was a great fan of 'Skippy the Bush Kangaroo' an old black and white TV series from Australia which seemed to be the top children's show in Turkmenistan. Elsewhere in the 'stans my passport caused officials to say 'Kewell' (an Australian footballer so well known to me that I had to google him to see how his name was spelt) to which I would nod and reply with 'Shane Warne' (a famous Australian cricketer) which would always cause some confused nodding.

The second check took much longer. I did not know the name of my guide; I just knew I was getting one, as that was a condition of entry. "No Guide, No Entry". Damn. I sat down and waited to see who would break first. What I did not know was that the Turkmen border had just been closed (borders close with alarming regularity for the slightest of reasons) and no one could enter from the Turkmenistan side, where my guide was trying to get in and rescue me. Using great initiative (and a packet of cigarettes) he had asked a soldier barring the way into the border post for a mobile phone number of one of the soldiers inside. It happened to be the Skippy fan, who delighted in rapidly escorting me through the visa process with the sour faced officials and outside to meet my guide. Welcome to Turkmenistan.

The Khojeli Crossing - I was dropped off by my guide/driver at the crossing, approximately 10 minutes from Konye-Urgench. After the fun and games I had had travelling into Turkmenistan I expected a similar long wait.

The border was closed, and had been for 2 days due to a dispute with the Uzbekistan military. Even with the rather unpredictable nature of border post openings and closings this was unusual. It was more of a diplomatic dispute this time. A massive queue of vehicles going back 3 km from the border gate welcomed us. My driver was going to turn around and drive to the Dashoguz crossing (although there were rumours this was closed too), about 3 hours east of where we were, but decided to ask the soldier at the gate whether it was worth waiting.

The soldier got very excited when he saw my passport. Australian passports, like the currency, are very colourful and full of drawings of all the cute and strange animals that inhabit the continent. He made a call, and then opened the gate, which caused a rush of people with their colourful bags to bear down on him. Raising his rifle into the air caused an immediate halt, and he gestured to me to walk through, before slamming and locking the gate again. The crowd was pretty unhappy at this turn of events, but rather selfishly I was delighted to be on the move again.

The process of leaving Turkmenistan could not be easier, I was the only person to be processed, and the soldiers and officials were bored after two days of inactivity. There was much laughter from the soldiers when one of them had to be dragged from watching a video on his computer to come and stamp my exit visa. The soldiers on the x-rays joked about me having guns and bombs in my luggage (only in Turkmenistan I thought) and whether I was in fact James Bond, trying on my Panama hat and swapping their peaked military hats with me. This was fun and games of a different sort, and a great way to leave the country.

Of course no bus was running across 'No mans land' and I had a long walk to a very confused Uzbekistan soldier napping at his post. I had to wake him so I could then go through a speedy record-breaking entry process, before heading off to find a taxi.

Costs and Money

Turkmenistan can be an expensive place, particularly if you have to drag a guide around with you. Hotel costs vary from **US$30 to US$250** depending on the quality of your room, although price does not always reflect that. Getting away from tour guides and planned itineraries brings the costs down considerably.

Local transport is cheap, whether that is by locals offering their cars as a taxi for a couple of dollars, or the amount that it would cost you to travel on local buses. Long distance transport is incredibly cheap, US$20 to fly from Ashgabat to anywhere in Turkmenistan, with journeys by rail costing under US$3. There are long distance buses too, which cost a similar amount.

Food and drink is very reasonable, particularly if you avoid hotels and the tourist traps that surround them. Eating at local restaurants and market stalls (always tasty and safe to eat) you will be hard pressed to spend US$5 per meal. Local beer costs US$1 to US$2 per bottle, half that price on draught, and vodka sets you back US$3 and upwards – there is a huge choice as you would expect from an ex-Soviet state.

Changing money

Do not use the Black market – it is basically the same as the official rate these days, and is not worth the added risks. Based on previous guidebooks recommending using the Black market to double your money, I went to the back of a Turkmenabad market, near the overflowing bins, soon after crossing from Uzbekistan. The process involved one person looking out for the police, while the other furtively counted out the Turkmen New Manat notes for me. I was certain, wrongly as it turned out, that I had been ripped off, and counted and re-counted the money, it was New Manat and not Manat as all other guidebooks had told me. I later met a tourist who had also changed money on the black market who was given worthless Old Manat. When I next changed money at the hotel in Ashgabat, I got exactly the same rate.

Turkmenistan New Manat Banknotes

Turkmenistan New Manat (TMT$) was introduced in 2009 to cope with the effects of hyperinflation, and is equivalent to the old Turkmenistan Manat on a basis of 1 Turkmenistan New Manat (TMT$) equaling 5,000 Turkmenistan Manat.

Notes are printed in denominations of 1, 5, 10, 20, 50, 100, and 500 TMT$.

Coins are 1, 2, 5, 10, 20 and 50 Tenge and 1 and 2 TM$.

As of June 2014, the rate you will get will be approximately TM$2.6 to the US$.

US$ notes are widely accepted. Credit cards are also accepted at most hotels, and up-market shops and restaurants.

What to buy

Good souvenirs are few and far between, and many come from China, or India. This is especially the case with carpets, particularly at the Tolkucha Bazaar, where almost everything is imported. There are some second-hand carpets sold by ladies in the hall just behind the entrance (and of course, as with all things in Turkmenistan, things change), haggling will be required.

The Ruhnama book. Available in all good book shops.

You do need an Export Permission Permit for any antique carpets purchased in a bazaar or private shop. The *Export Commission* at the back of the *Carpet Museum* in Ashgabat (phone 398879 and 398887, opening hours Mon to Fri 2.30PM to 5.30PM, Sat 10 to 12AM) has to certify that the carpet is not more than 50 years old and may be exported. The permit cost is based on the size of the carpet, and includes certification and export duty, payable in US$.

Why not add to your own despots library by adding Turkmenbashi's self-penned Ruhnama book, exploring his views on what it means to be a Turkmen. Surprisingly, this is a fairly sensible read. Purchase it for TM$7 from state bookshops, the large stores are located near the university.

Other souvenirs you can buy include plates with an eye on them, and also string bracelets with a knot in them (both to ward off the dangers of the evil eye), copies of Turkmen neck jewellery, and the local vodka.

All bags are x-rayed and thoroughly searched so no antiquities should be exported.

Far Flung Tip:

Bribes: Packets of cigarettes are a great way of adding to the income of police, and speeding up processing in airports and border crossings. They only cost approx U$1 for a packet of 20, and guarantee a smooth and easy passage with no questions.

Photography

Turkmenistan does not actively encourage tourism. Not unsurprisingly, there are considerable misunderstandings over how tourists, and their desire to take photographs, should be treated. I asked my guide if I could photograph all buildings and people including the army and police, aware that other older travel guides had said this was prohibited. The reply was "Yes, no problem."

Passing the Presidential palace in Ashgabat I asked to slow down to take a photo of the massive white edifice with a gold dome. "Not allowed", the driver shouted and sped up. Later, at the Independence monument I was taking a photo of the soldiers standing guard. As soon as my camera was out we were jumped upon by four other soldiers waving their arms and pointing at my camera. I asked my guide again about the rules, and he just smiled and shrugged his shoulders.

The rules are ill defined, but to generalise: Avoid taking photographs of government buildings (including the airport) and members of the police and military.

At many historical sites there is an extra charge for bringing in cameras, usually between 5TM$and 10TM$.

Electricity

Turkmenistan runs on 220 Volt , 50 AC, with a twin round pin plug (similar to France and Germany). Note that the sockets are often recessed and round, and not all adaptors will fit.

Internet Access

To sum it up in one word: appalling. The Internet is tightly controlled and censored in Turkmenistan. Obviously this can change at the flick of a switch, but currently the following sites are blocked:

- Facebook, so do not expect to update while travelling!

- Twitter

- Tumblr

- Youtube

- Google+ websites (although Google itself does work, not that you can access many of the result pages)

- Websites from countries that do not get on with Turkmenistan

- Websites from countries that do get on with Turkmenistan (Uzbekistan for example, frustratingly as I was travelling there next).

- Websites that criticise Turkmenistan,

- Random web sites that have nothing to do with Turkmenistan.

Attachments to emails do not always work, this is not a speed issue, again it is some form of censorship. It seemed to be 50/50 as to whether a download would work. Surprisingly, pornography, did not seem to be censored (it had to be tested!) which shows where the censors see the danger. Censorship is not done to protect the people from graphic and upsetting content or from time wasting (hello Facebook), but to protect the government from mass organization against it. There is a real fear of an Arab Spring-like uprising. By suppressing and controlling internet access they think they can prevent this. You can but try.

Despite all utilities such as water and electricity being connected and supplied free to all Turkmen citizens, Internet access connection is charged at an extreme premium, with a DSL connection costing up to

US$7000 for the average householder (government employees get a significant discount).

Access to wi-fi is pitiful. Hotels and the shopping centres advertise it, but often it is not working, or it is too slow to be able to synchronize mail with your email provider. Use web mail to access your email if possible.

3G and 4G roaming is possible on an international phone, all the above sites are blocked, and speed is particularly intermittent. Check with your phone provider before leaving on exactly how much you are charged per megabyte downloaded, it could be awfully expensive.

Far Flung Tip:

Fast uncensored Internet: is available at the US embassy to all. The Public Affairs section of the US Embassy on the fourth floor of the *Alk Alytn Hotel*, 141/1, Magumguly Avenue.

The US Embassy is open to all friendly nations. Inside I met Russians, Germans and an Azerbaijani amongst others, so imagine maybe only North Koreans are not welcome. **Open from 9AM to 5PM Monday to Friday, and 9AM to 12PM on Saturdays**. You need your passport, and have to pass through a metal detector, and then have your Internet device scanned in an X Ray machine. There are comfy chairs and couches to sit on, and free coffee and tea to drink, although the large lounge area is often full of local Turkmen teenagers accessing Facebook and Youtube, or successfully looking in amazement at previously blocked google pages.

This is the real benefit from staying at the All Alytyn Hotel when in Ashgabat. With your logon and password you can wander by when you want, relax on the carpet on the fourth floor (bring a pillow from your room to rest on), and access free uncensored Internet at any time. And then you leave for another part of Turkmenistan and enter the Internet black hole again.

Health and Safety

You can walk right up the 'Gates of Hell' gas crater in Derweze and jump or fall in. There is no safety barrier, no warnings, and this goes for life in general in Turkmenistan. You have to look after yourself.

The biggest problem you may face, on the second or third day, is a stomach reaction to local germs. No matter how careful you are, peeling all fruit and drinking mineral water (do not drink the tap water, it is laced with heavy metals and bacteria, and avoid ice in drinks) you will come into contact with some germs that will send you to the toilet regularly. Consult a travel doctor before you depart for advice on how to deal with issues that might arise.

Bottled water is widely available, and often given free in hotels.

Vaccinations against diphtheria, tetanus, polio, hepatitis A and B are recommended. A vaccination against typhus is also recommended in case you stay in poor unhygienic conditions, and a vaccination against rabies should be considered, avoid being friendly with dogs or camels.

Not all medicines are easily available, bring your own and do not expect to be able to buy any international brands.

Do not discuss politics with anyone you meet, for their benefit as much as yours. Critics of the government fill Turkmenistan's prisons.

The police can be corrupt, and will ask for fines for crossing roads, even on the green pedestrian light, or for taking photographs. In most countries I would suggest you fight this, but in Turkmenistan it is not worth it. The police will be happy with US$2 or a packet of cigarettes. This is much preferable to being taken to a police station and having to argue your case, wasting valuable hours.

Prostitution is an underground industry, but is highly illegal, particularly with foreigners. The police will delight in exacting large fines (bribes) if they find a tourist with a prostitute.

Homosexuality is considered a very serious crime in Turkmenistan. The regular punishment is two years in a Turkmen jail.

Security

Thanks to the ubiquitous police on every corner, crime is rare, and against foreigners even rarer still. You can wander around at night without worrying, most areas are very brightly lit anyway. You will be stopped and possibly arrested (and certainly fined) by the police **after 11PM, when there is a curfew.**

Turkmenistan is a country which fulfils the adage of early to bed, early to rise. Ensure you keep your passport and travel pass, or copies of them, with you when you are outside your hotel.

Travel is limited to areas allowed by the government, defined in your travel documents. All travel near the Afghanistan border is forbidden. Roadblocks are a way of life. Accept them and the possible delays you may face when travelling between cities by road.

Use common sense as always, and follow any travel warnings from your embassy about Turkmenistan.

Travel Insurance

Get some. You are crazy to travel in Central Asia without comprehensive travel insurance including air evacuation. Hospitals in Ashgabat are actually quite good, although not up to western standard, and this is despite the Ruhnama being used as the basic text in medical teaching in the very recent past. Outside of the capital the medical facilities are poor, and best avoided.

The number for the local ambulance service in case of an **emergency is 03.** Please note however that the operator may only speak Russian or Turkmen.

Vinyl making a comeback. Used in the preparation of Non Bread

Food and Drink

A street shaslyk vendor in Ashgabat

Turkmen Food

Meat and bread dominate the diet as in much of Central Asia. Lamb, beef and chicken are available on almost all menus. Shashlyk (Kebabs) and meat and vegetable pastry Somsa (Samosa) are available from roadside stalls, bazaars and local restaurants.

Plov, also the national dish of Uzbekistan, is a very filling meal usually only available at lunchtimes. It is growing in international popularity and is now served up in posh New York and London restaurants. Each region cooks it their own style, but the staples are chunks of meat, lamb or beef, with fat attached, being cooked over several

Plov being prepared in a huge wok.

hours alongside carrots, onions and lots of rice in a massive cauldron. The fat permeates the rice giving it a distinctive taste, which makes Plov very tasty and filling, albeit not the healthiest choice for a meal. Turkmen food is not spicy, but can be heavily salted, particularly Plov.

Russian influenced food, particularly sturgeon and meat and vegetable soups, can be found in many restaurants.

Meals are almost always accompanied with Non bread, similar to Indian Nan bread, although stodgier. Baked in tandoor ovens first thing in the morning, and without additives, so buy it early and eat it while it is still warm! By night time the bread can be quite stale. Uzbek Non bread is commonly thought to better than the traditional Turkmen variety, and the best bakers in the Turkmen city are Uzbeks on working visas.

Fresh Non bread just pulled from the Tandoor.

Because of its vital importance at times of famine, Non bread plays an important part in Turkmen culture. It should be treated with respect, and not dropped on the floor, turned upside down, or thrown away, to avoid upsetting your hosts or fellow diners.

Vegetarian food can be obtained, but it is difficult. Turkmen do not truly understand the concept of vegetarianism, and will often add minced meat into any vegetable dish you order. The ready alternative is to make your own meals from the wonderful selections of seasonal vegetables available in each city's markets, or grocery shops.

Seasonal fruit from the markets is a delight to view, photograph, view, photograph, and to eat. Wash and indulge in fat juicy Shiraz grapes, huge oranges, and the many varieties of melons. Melon is considered the national fruit, with claims of over 400 different varieties.

Fresh dough before being rolled and put in the Tandoor to make Non bread.

Drink

Non Alcoholic

Green Tea (Chai) is the national drink; black tea runs it a close second. Available everywhere, even in the street, tea sellers will dispense their wares to passing pedestrians. It often has milk added, particularly if the drinker is a Westerner.

Camel's milk (Chal) is a more up market beverage. Fizzy due to it being fermented, it has an extremely sour taste and is a considered a delicacy.

Mineral Water- Available everywhere.

Alcoholic Beverages

Beer – Available throughout the country in glass and plastic bottles, and occasionally, in hotels and restaurants, on draught. The national brew is delightfully called *'Berk'* – "Hi Waiter, Berk (slight pause) please". Unfortunately it is not very nice, low in alcohol at 2.8%, and very sweet. A great hop-infused nose destroyed by its' oh so sweet taste. There seems to be an intention to make up for the lack of alcohol by adding sugar.

'Barlos' is the light beer alternative, if Berk is not light enough for you. 1.8% alcohol and packed to the gills with even more sugar for extreme sweetness. The only beer I had to pour down the drain in Turkmenistan. Avoid.

The good news is there is another delightfully named beer *'Di-Zi'* maybe referring to the after effects of having too many. It comes in 1.5 litre bottles. A healthy 4.5% alcohol, great hoppy taste, no sweetness and similar to a German Pilsener. A great drink, but sadly not as widely available as the two other local brews.

'Pulsar' is available in Ashgabat, and bottle shops in Mary and Turkmenabad. It is an excellent Uzbekistan brew from Samarkand. 4.2% alcohol, great taste, and actually brewed with German help using

Reinheitsgebot brewing purity method. If you are ever in Samarkand get it on draught, possibly the best beer I have tasted in Central Asia.

Imports from Turkey, Russia and Europe are available at extortionate prices, buy local as much as possible.

Probably the best named beers in the world. Turkmenistan Beers.

Vodka remains the most popular drink, and it is available everywhere, even sold alongside newspapers in street kiosks. Seriously cheap, it costs less than bottled water which I always find hard to comprehend. The cheaper stuff tastes like rocket fuel, but spending only US$2 gives you a 375ml bottle which is surprisingly drinkable. Go into a bottle shop and you will be presented with over 100 different varieties, most of them distilled in Turkmenistan, a vodka drinker's paradise.

Wine is available, but despite the abundance of Shiraz grapes, is not of great quality. It is expensive, and only a dollar or two less than the French or Spanish imported variety. Surprisingly, or not if you tried the 'Berk' beer, it is very sweet to taste. I sampled a few local varieties, which were mostly red, but all were too sweet for my palate.

Turkmenistan: Places to visit

An Imam at the Mausolea of Ashkab, Merv

Pilgrims at the Turabeg Khanum Mausoleum, Gurganj

Turkmenabad

Camels in the Karakum desert outside Turkmenabad

If arriving from Uzbekistan and the Farab border crossing you will go to Turkmenabad (also known as Turkmenabat, and until changed by the President in 1999, Charjou), the second largest city in Turkmenistan, with a population of 250,000. On the way you have to cross the Amu Daryu River, the famed Oxus River of antiquity, which is done via a military pontoon bridge with tolls and police checkpoints at either end.

This was quite a surprise, I expected a normal bridge with pylons, and not something left over from the Second World War. As it is a major river thoroughfare tugs are used to unpin sections of the pontoon to allow ships past, luckily not while I was crossing.

After a few days you get used to the military checkpoints everywhere. Even in the most remote parts of the Kara Kum desert they will appear as if a mirage with no buildings, or indeed other traffic, around. They are always happy to delay your journey and make a small profit where possible.

Turkmenabad itself is an industrial sprawl, with none of its ancient buildings remaining. It was an important Soviet industrial city, manufacturing cars, textiles and processing food, however in recent times it has fallen on hard times. Much of the industry has relocated to either Russia or Ashgabat since independence. My guide admitted that there was not much to see or do there, apart from a few parks, even the local cinemas had recently closed.

The drab industrial streets were distinguished only by the golden statues of Niyazov adorning every public building. My guide, Alexi, did not know of a single place a tourist should go, and he lived there. It is a place you arrive in, refuel, change money (though not at the black market), and visit the sites outside the city, or drive on to either Ashgabat or Mary.

Pressing Alexi again on the one place he would like to show off in the city, he reluctantly took me to the central market, Dunya Bazaar. A Soviet edifice with glass covered lanes of produce and shops. In the food hall area there were lots of interesting looking food stalls, loaded with kebabs and bread. I ordered a very tasty kebab for TM$5 and a huge bottle of local beer for TM$2.

Travel

Fly: Turkmenabad airport had daily flights to Ashgabat and Mary (approximate cost is US$15 to US$20). Usually you can get a seat, but contact a travel agent beforehand to book you a seat (see the list of travel agents in Appendix II).

Train: Trains run twice a day to Ashgabat and Mary (US$4) although they can be fully booked up to five days in advance. Again, these can be booked for you by a travel agent.

Coach and Mini Bus: run to Ashgabat and Mary, and leave from in front of the Railway station (US$2 – US$4). They depart when full.

Taxi: to and from the Farab border post with Uzbekistan. Cost is approximately US$30, less if shared.

I had chosen to drive the six hours to Merv, to see a little more of the country and be able to stop and explore ancient settlements. It is a long journey, and is perfect to give an the idea of how much of Turkmenistan is desert, but after an hour or two of sand, more sand, oil and gas wells, and more sand, the journey does tire a bit. I would recommend going by train or plane, unless you want to see camels in the wild.

Where to Stay

Hotel Amu Darja, Nijazov köcesi 14 (US$70 Room) Basic hotel, expensive but there is little competition. Popular with travellers.

Jeyhun Hotel, 106, Bitarap Street. (US$60 Room).

Turkmenabat Hotel, Magtymguy Dayoli Street (US$45 Room)

Things to See in Turkmenabad

The real areas of interest are outside of Turkmenabad. So little of the original buildings remain, that these attractions are likely to only be of interest to the most obsessive Silk Road aficionado.

Amul

An ancient Silk Road city which became a transport hub on the Amu Darya River, as it linked Merv to Bukhara and Khiva.

A fortress, palace, houses, and a prison were located here, until destroyed by Genghis Khan in 1220. Now there is very little left, much of the mud brick walls have been eroded by time, and, in the past, into the kilns of a brick factory built on the site. Located ten km from Turkmenabad, the sprawl of the city has encroached and built over much of the site, which has yet to be fully excavated.

Caravanserai Dayakhatyn

On the road to Khorsem, two hours from Turkmenabad are the ruins of a Silk Road Caravanserai, a rest point for weary travelers where they could feed their camels, have a beer, and sleep. There is more to see here than Amul, but most lies in ruins. The main archway, and remnants of domes of the housing can be seen, along with the stabling quarters.

Koytendag Nature Reserve

Six hours from Turkmenabad, formerly known as the Kugintag nature reserve, a special permit is required to enter. Alongside beautiful mountain climbs and an endangered wild goat, the key attraction is the Dinosaur plateau, where over 400 footprints left in limestone have been preserved. Only recently discovered in the 1980's, they are an impressive sight, with some footprints larger than 1.5 meters in length.

Mary

View towards the Garbanguly Hajji Mosque in Mary

Formerly known as Merv, and to be honest, that was a much better name. Saying you are "off to Mary for the weekend" invites too many questions and blank looks, at least outside of Turkmenistan.

Mary is the fourth largest city in Turkmenistan with approximately 140,000 inhabitants. Both it and Turkmenabad are tiny compared with Ashgabat, which dominates in population, activities and importance.

The locals I talked to in Mary all had plans to move to Ashgabat in the near future, the younger people in particular were extremely bored and dreamed of skateboarding in the one official skateboard park in Ashgabat. Mary had no such luxuries and the best places to skateboard were on the marble steps of the museum and mosque, both of which resulted in being chased by police within minutes (lasting the longest before being chased away was considered a Badge of Honour by the skateboarders).

Mary was an oasis city on the Silk Road, and today is still surrounded totally by the Kara Kum desert.

Tourists come here as it is the best place to stay to explore the ancient city of Merv, approximately 20km from the modern city.

Travel

Fly: Four flights a day to Ashgabat. The modern air terminal is midway between Merv and Mary, making it possible to do a (rushed) day trip to the ruined city. Tickets are ludicrously cheap, subsidised even for foreigners, at US15 each way.

Train: The railway station is on the Eastern side of Mary. Trains run three times a day to Ashgabat, and twice a day to Turkmenabad. This is slower than driving, probably because the heat of the desert damages the rail lines. Trains are very crowded, and are often full five days before departure.

Coach and Minibus: Run to Ashgabat and Turkmenabad, (both approx 6 hours away) and leave from in front of the railway station (US$2 – US$4). They depart when full.

Where to Stay

Almost inevitably you will end up in the **Margush Hotel** (cost approx US$60), the only major hotel in Mary.

There is a Motel, the **Rahat**, at approximately $10 cheaper, but it is on the edge of the city, and you might as well stay in the city to explore it.

A hostel is located opposite the railway station with shared dormitories, although as a tourist you may be turned away.

The Margush is very central, right next to the Main Mosque and the City Museum. Initially it impresses with its modern visage of mirrored glass and metal, but inside is a terrible disappointment. I have never seen a dirtier stained carpet in any hotel I have stayed in (and I have been in some real dumps), and the Margush is supposed to be a 4 star hotel. I had to move my bedroom initially as the air-conditioning sounded like a column of tanks continually passing overhead. Luckily this was not a problem, as only two other people seemed to be staying there. I did get a good night's sleep in my new room, so I count that as a major plus point.

The bar is overpriced, only stocking foreign beers at foreign prices. Dinner is served there, but there is great food a short walk away and based on my breakfast experience (2 boiled eggs and 2 slices of chocolate cake, an interesting culinary mix) would not be worth investigating.

Where to Eat

Tandoor Kitchen: Leaving the Margush walk to your left, towards the city. You will pass a tennis court, then turn left again and you will be on a footpath alongside the Murghab River. Walk along this, passing occasional stray dogs and children and you will come to a bridge. Cross this and you will be standing next to the *Tandoor Kitchen* a large outdoor kitchen, with massive tandoors and flames being thrown skyward from the kebab grills **(at least if you are there after 6PM).**

The open kitchen (there is no roof or seating) is the place to eat, judging by the huge queues of people who constantly arrived, waited and collected their food, from policemen, an old imam, to business men sweltering in their suits. No English is spoken here, but that is really not a problem. Everyone orders the samosas, a beautifully cooked parcel of vegetables and minced lamb costing TM$1 each, or the lamb kebabs at TM$2 each. Surprisingly in this meat loving land, vegetarian samosas are also available, at the same price. You can collect your food and sit down by the Margush river to eat.

Behind the *Tandoor Kitchen* are a few shops selling basics necessities, including beer (TM$4 for a litre), vodka (TM$6 for a bottle), as well as local pistachio nuts (TM$3 for 250 grams), which made for a nice dessert.

There is also a pizza kitchen, which was empty at the time and looked rather overpriced on the menu posted in English outside.

Things to See in Mary

Apart from the usual golden statues of Niyazov, and white marble clad government buildings, Mary has got more than enough to keep you occupied for a day.

National History and Ethnology Museum

On Mollanepes Shayoly. Expensive at TM$35 (locals pay TM$5), this modern museum has a huge number of displays. It is too huge by far, as it tries to cover too much; ancient history, natural history and modern history with differing quality of exhibits.

Some of the beautiful archaeological discoveries from Merv and the Margush settlement (a Bronze Age site nearby) are worth the price of admission, in particular the pottery, small statues, and coins and carved and engraved elephant tusks, but case after case full of stuffed birds weary after a while.

There are also larger galleries devoted to many photographs of the current leader with world dignitaries in a variety of interesting costumes. Be very selective in what you see, unless your interest is ornithology or Gurbanguly Berdimuhamedow.

Gurbanguly Hajji Mosque

On Mollanepes Shayoly. A rather beautiful white marble and blue domed mosque built in 2009. Named after the current leader (he is starting to get his name on things). Only open at set prayer times.

Central Bazaar

On Mollanepes Shayoly. If you are in Turkmenistan for any period of time, you will always end up at a Bazaar, basically a large market selling anything you could want to buy, providing it is imported from China or grown locally. The one in Mary gives you a fascinating insight into the lives of locals. Sure, there are also the normal piles of imported Chinese toys and home wares.

On the Mezzanine between the food and bridal wear floors is a cool little music shop. Although packed with pirated music from Bon Jovi, the Scorpions and Michael Learns to Rock (why is this band so popular in far flung places? I never see them in any other store, but wander into a wooden shack in Papua New Guinea, or a tiny shop in Bohol in the Philippines, and you are confronted by all their recorded output, which always seems to be rather excessive, even for lovers of Danish soft pop music). To one side is a case packed with Turkmen artists. This is great for picking up some unique local music as a souvenir, or as a gift for a music lover. 90% is cassette, 10% is CD. Cassettes are coming back in fashion didn't you know?

Far Flung Tip:

The spectacular wedding shop on the second floor of the Central Bazaar is worth a visit. Not just because it is air-conditioned, but it has an intriguing display of wedding outfits to be worn by the bride and groom. Many are exotic; one of the most memorable was a cross between Turkish belly dancer and Scottish Hogmanay wear. Some of the dresses are festooned with so many bronze plates you wonder how the poor bride could stand up. Even better, you get to see the soon to be married couples being measured and trying on the outfits.

On the ground floor are the aisles of fresh vegetables and fruits from the nearby-irrigated desert. Sadly the roof has no skylights, or even artificial lighting, shrouding the bustling and colourful stalls and produce in semi darkness. Poor for photography, still great for snacking on fresh fruit though (peel it, or wash it, as always to avoid Turkmen belly lurgy).

The choice is limited by what is in season, no oranges flown in from Florida here. The grapes in particular were tasty and dripping with juice.

At the edge of the Bazaar is a small shop selling ice cream. Only a very few flavours are available, all home made. The electricity supply was consistent when I was in Mary, so I risked buying a cone of the more unusual pistachio flavour.   Chocolate, vanilla and fruit were the other choices. It was absolutely delicious on a hot day.

The Russian Orthodox Church, Pokrpyvska, in Mary.

Pokrpyvska Russian Orthodox Church

On Seydi Kochesi. A throwback to Soviet times, covered wall to wall in icons, and disturbingly graphic religious imagery, as is the Orthodox way. An old priest with a beard as flowing as his robes will follow you around, either contemplating whether to try and convert you, or to stop you stealing the valuable icons.

Russian Mig 29 Plane

On Seydi Kochesi. A rather stunning looking military plane incongruously dumped on a plinth in a residential street near the Russian Orthodox

Mig 29 Fighter Plane on a Mary city street.

Church. The locals I had talked to had no idea of its existence, and it was only by luck I came across it as I left the church.

Murghab Boat Trips

Niyazov Central Park. On the pontoon beneath the Fun Fair, tickets can be purchased from the fair ticket booths even when the fair is closed. These are the typical pedal boats found in lakes around the world. Great for travelling down the Murghab and seeing a different perspective on Mary, although with the speed the river was moving while I was there you would not want to paddle up stream for very long, or fall into the murky water.

Mary Fun Fair

Niyazov Central Park. The 'Fun' Fair is possibly misnamed judging by the state of it. This is in a small park next to the Bazaar and enclosed by the Murghab River. It has been here since Soviet times, and it shows. Rusty securing pylons on the big wheel were being covered in layer after layer of green paint when we visited there, thirty minutes before opening at 6PM.

I had managed to pick up a small entourage of teenagers by this point, and even they thought it was not safe. Cheap at TM$1 per ride, you get what you pay for. The dodgems did look cool, but the tiny area they were on meant that you would barely be able to move a metre before crashing into another dodgem. Although, perhaps that is the point.

The Kara Kum desert which covers most of Turkmenistan

The ancient city of Merv

Ancient protective Mud walls in the city of Merv

Merv is the real reason you travel to Mary, not the Fun Park or the MIG plane, exciting as they are.

History of Merv

Merv was the largest city on earth in the twelfth century, with over a million inhabitants, a major trading post on the Silk Road, and acting as a bulwark against forces coming from Afghanistan (some things don't change).

First settled in the 3rd century BC, it expanded with each new leader, from Alexander the Great, who renamed it after himself, to the Arabs, and then the Turks. It spread out for 100 km, close to the Afghan border, each new occupying force building a new city so that it gradually expanded.

The Mausoleum of Sultan Sanjar rises from the desert in Merv.

Like so many other cities in central Asia it felt the wrath of Genghis Khan, who laid waste to it in 1220, with reports of each Mongol soldier massacring 400 men, women and children.

It never really recovered from this onslaught and dwindled as it became fought over by the Emirs of Bukhara and the Persians, a final victory in 1785 by the Emir Shah Murad led to the last 100,000 inhabitants being deported to an oasis near Bukhara.

In 2001 it was declared a UNESCO site, and is now a place frequented more by archaeologists than tourists.

Travel

You will normally have a guide/driver, or be on a tour, unless the rules change. A taxi costs approx US$20 for the journey or US$50 for 6 hours (go for the six hours or longer). The city is large that it is very hard to see without a car. The journey from Mary, passes a rather spectacular horse racing stadium built in the desert (the current President loves horses apparently) before arriving at Merv after approximately thirty minutes. If you are lucky you will only be stopped at police roadblocks twice.

Hiring a Guide

Do get a guide if you can, Yevgenia Golubeva, who used to manage many of the archaeological digs, comes highly recommended. I do not have a current number for her (there is one in the Lonely Planet but it is years out of date), but the Mary National History and Ethnology Museum, where she still works part-time, can give you her contact details. The travel company booking your tour before departure should also be able to book her. **Cost is approx US$80 for the day**.

I was lucky I did not need a guide this time. During my travels through Mary on the previous day I met and chatted to a number of locals, who wanted to try out their English or work out what this Panama hat-wearing foreigner was up to wandering around the Bazaar. Suarev, a 17-year-old blonde skateboarder with good English, learnt from deciphering the lyrics to songs from American punk bands. He had a penchant for overusing swear words and dreamed of moving to Ashgabat to try out the skate park there. He was excited I had heard of Green Day and The Offspring, and called his girlfriend and her friends over as we explored for the MIG fighter plane in Mary. All were equally astonished that such a weird thing existed in their city, although they were equally excited, and more disturbed, by the contents of the Russian Orthodox Church, and kept looking back over their shoulder in fear at the priest trailing behind us.

Suarev's girlfriend was from Ashgabat, and was on holiday here with her mother, Alianna*. Alianna was a senior member of a government body in charge of oil and gas exploration, at the heart of Turkmenistan's economic growth. And she also loved history, having studied it at universities in Moscow and Ashgabat. I persuaded my driver to go to Bayramaly, on the edge of Merv, where the family was staying with their mother for a holiday, and pick Alianna up to be my expert guide for the day.

* All names have been changed

Entry Fee

Admittance is TMN$22, and there is a very small museum by the ticket booth, which has a few antiquities inside and a rather nice scaled model of the main part of Merv.

Remote and rarely visited, the vast site has many superb remains of forts, city walls, ice stores, and houses of the inhabitants. It has hard to imagine how the largest city on earth can be reduced to ruins, just dirt and mud, and no inhabitants. It is a city and story few know about.

With the help of a four wheel-drive car, (a car is needed, the site is vast) and many bottles of water, I spent the whole day uncovering what it was like to live in this abandoned city. By afternoon I was exhausted by the desert temperatures and the distances traveled. Only the ubiquitous wandering camels were enjoying the heat. I could easily have spent more days exploring one of the more unknown, but well-preserved, Silk Road cities.

Things to See in Merv

Greater Gyzgala

The fortress of Great Gyzgala at Merv

A fortress with high corrugated walls made of clay. An unusual windowless castle just outside the city wall, and the best preserved of all buildings in Merv. This was part of Soltangala, a city established by Abu Muslim around the 7th Century BC. There were many of these buildings, known as Kushk, which roughly translates to pavilion, dotted around the city.

They were fortified palaces, where the very rich or important lived. The first story was used for storage of food and weapons. The second story was where the living quarters were located. Parapets on the top of the walls made it distinctive and defendable, and it is possible that more living quarters were based here, using tents.

The literal translation of Gyzgala is 'Girls Castle'. The story is told that over forty girls were hiding there when the Mongols attacked Merv. When they saw the devastation the Mongols were causing on their city, they held hands and jumped to their deaths from its walls.

The Greater Gyzgala had 17 rooms in it, surrounding a central courtyard. A short walk beyond is a smaller less well-preserved Kushk, the Lesser Gyzgala, which you can walk around and see how thick the defensive mud brick walls were. It is in ruins, take care not to disturb the remaining mud bricks. Although few visitors come here their impact through climbing on the walls and etching graffiti is all too obvious.

The Greater Gyzgala is now fenced off to aid preservation and is easy to walk. Go here first in the morning when the sun is shining directly on the walls for the best photographs.

Gawurgala

The gate and buildings of the wall around the city can be seen here, as if cut away for a 3D drawing. This city was established by the Greeks around 400BC, during the Hellenistic era under the rule of the King Antiochus I, and became more important under the Persians during Islam's first two centuries.

You can actually see how the city walls were expanded to deal with advances in firepower. First on the left is the smaller mud brick wall, built upon with larger bricks for the second expansion, before a larger and higher mud brick wall, with a platform for artillery, was built on the right.

The size of the wall shows the importance of Merv at this time. No other excavated city of this time period has been discovered to have such large walls.

The city walls of Gawurgala at Merv.

Inside the city nothing remains to be seen, although it is now regularly occupied by archaeologists as excavations produce an enormous amount of material about its occupants and their lives.

Walking up and over the walls is a fairly easy climb, although I would avoid walking over the actual excavated remains shown in the photograph. Mainly because they are mud brick, and the elements are already slowly destroying them without human intervention, and because the climb is steep and covered with tiny balls of mud acting like marbles underfoot. Add to this the lack of hand-holds and you have the perfect opportunity to watch a tourist go head over heels numerous times to the bottom. The local we observed doing this was a bit bloodied and shaken, but was not badly injured through luck. You have been warned.

Zoroastrian Ice House

The Zoroastrian Ice House at Merv.

A 12th-century construction, approximately 30 meters in circumference, it is well preserved and worth visiting. Ice, as well as fire was an important element in the Zoroastrian religion which grew and flourished here, as Merv became one of the most important cities on the Silk Road.

Mausoleum of Sultan Sanjar

This mausoleum has been rebuilt since its original construction in the 12th century, although the interior is largely intact. Sadly a lot of its distinctive features were lost in the 1990s as the rush job to ensure it did not collapse removed many of its unique features and replaced them with additions thought up by the Russian architect.

It is a distinctive square shape, standing out clearly in the surrounding desert and was supposed to be visible a day's march away. Today many pilgrims visit, some prostrating themselves on the ground before it, and dragging themselves inside it.

Even on the hottest days the dome and thick walls keep it cool, and it is a great place to rest after clambering around the other sites of Merv, engaging in people watching and marveling at the small birds that fly at speed around the dome.

Erk Kala

The city of Alexandra the Great. There is a nice climb up from the road to the top of the fifty metre defensive wall surrounding this city built in the 3rd century BC. Nothing physical remains to be seen here, except for the sand and earth covered walls, although this in itself is impressive.

They are still large and powerful reaching a height of thirty metres. Inside the fortress is an area of over 20 hectares, much is still hidden beneath the soil, including the remains of the palace, barracks, city buildings and main square where the population gathered to hear proclamations and witness executions. Observing it from the air would make it even more remarkable, as the sheer size of the city could be easily seen. A favourite site for British Museum archaeological digs in the colder months. You may bump into members of the dig and learn just how much more remains to be discovered.

Mausolea of the Two Ashkab

The black marble cenotaphs are contained in two small-reconstructed buildings in front of larger, and also reconstructed, temples. These are the resting places of Al Hakim Ibn Amr Al Jafari and Buraida Ibn Al Huseib Al Islami. They were two companions of the Prophet Mohammed. If you are a Muslim in Turkmenistan this is the reason you would visit Merv. The site is packed all day long, and hawkers jostle with the faithful in selling various holy items, as well as the ubiquitous string bracelets to ward off the evil eye. The faithful, dressed in fine clothes, walk around each mausoleum three times, before departing again to their cars.

Just outside the Mausolea is an unusual cemetery with each tomb resembling a small house. These plots on a small hill are highly sought after, as they are so close to the Ashkab, and effort has gone into each tomb's design to make them individual and impressive.

Nearby an old part of the city wall there is a tree covered in string bracelets that are designed to ward the off the evil eye from whoever placed them there. Islam is the dominant religion, but some ancient beliefs are very strong.

Bayramaly

The modern city of Bayramaly is built on the ruins, and encroaching ever closer. Parts of old city walls can be seen interspersed with modern housing. Many of the small houses here have small vegetable gardens, and even minor disturbance of the earth still gives up many treasures. After exploring Merv I had dinner with my guide Alianna, whose mother lived there, and her mantelpiece was covered in small jars, arrow heads, and bones she had uncovered while planting potatoes.

Ashgabat

Peak hour on the highways in central Ashgabat.

Ashgabat is the capital of Turkmenistan, with a population of over one million. Constant immigration into the city from the outside cities and rural areas of Turkmenistan will continue to see this number increase.

The city is situated beneath the Kopeg Dag mountain range, which forms the border with Iran. It is, like most places in Turkmenistan, surrounded by desert and can suffer sandstorms at any time of the year.

Located close to Nissa, the ancient Parthian capital, it is a relatively new city founded by the Russians in 1881. A major earthquake, 7.1 on the Richter scale, caused massive damage and casualties in 1948. Soviet censorship prevented the outside world knowing how bad the disaster was, but estimates suggest upwards of 170,000 people (over half the population at that time) may have been killed.

Many of those buildings that survived the earthquake have since been destroyed as part of Niyazov's grand plan to show the rebirth of Ashgabat as a modern world city. Massive marble-clad government and apartment buildings have replaced the original Tsarist and early communist buildings. Locals are still unhappy with this, despite many of the old buildings that were destroyed being in a poor state of repair and lacking modern amenities like hot water. The new apartments are too expensive for them to buy, and whole communities have been dispersed to the edges of Ashgabat.

This has also resulted in the centre of Ashgabat being reminiscent of North Korea and the highways built with no cars to travel on them. Ashgabat has the cars, but few people have reason to travel to the centre and most apartment buildings remain empty. Prices, controlled by the government, have recently been slashed. A modern 2 bedroom apartment with all utilities paid will now cost under US$1000 a month, with further reductions for government employees, but still few choose to live in a place which has government building as neighbours, with few restaurants or recreational facilities.

Despite the attractions of cheap petrol, the roads in the centre of Ashgabat are deserted much of the time. The generous multi-lane highways remain empty, while the suburbs and the older parts of Ashgabat, have traditional single-lane potholed roads.

Still, building huge highways is a great way to spend money, and it looks mightily impressive. In February 2014 Berdimuhamedow made public his plans for a subway system for Ashgabat, a new way to spend vast amounts of cash, import more white marble from Italy, and somewhat unnecessary for a city with massive empty roads, which also happens to be earthquake prone.

Travel:

Fly: Saparmurat Turkmenbashy airport is a 30-minute drive from the city centre, handling both international and domestic flights. A taxi to the city costs TM$20. Note a new airport is being built next door, and is planned to open in 2014/2015 to celebrate the Central Asian games.

Train: The main railway station is on Gurbansoltan-eje Avenue. From here you can travel to Mary, Turkmenabad, Balkanabad and Dashoguz (if you have the right permits). Trains are very crowded, and are often full five days before departure.

Coach and Mini Bus: Run to all cities in Turkmenistan. They arrive and depart from the stands on the left side of the main railway station. They depart when full.

Where to Stay

Ashgabat has the best accommodation in Turkmenistan, which ranges from mid price to expensive. There is a boom in hotel building, maybe to house foreign oil and natural gas engineers, so expect more choices when you arrive.

Here are a selected number of hotels:

Independent Hotel.
33, Novoarchabilsk Street. US$50 per night. Modern, more motel-like, includes swimming pool and (small) inside tennis court which is a bit unusual. 10km from the city.

Lachin Hotel

589, Bitarap Street,. US$60 per night. More of a business hotel, 3km from the city.

Ak Altyn Hotel

141/1, Magumguly Avenue US$80 per night. In Soviet times the only hotel available for tourists and showing its age slightly. It is recommended due to its location, 2km walk to the centre, with lots of good eating places around, and also because of the location of the US embassy on level four.

In most countries you might have second thoughts about sleeping beneath, or on top of, a US embassy but this has to be weighed against the fourth floor being the only place you can get fast uncensored wi-fi in Turkmenistan. This is a huge plus point! See the section on Internet access at the start of this guide.

Note: if you are genuinely worried about security, with Iran being only 20km and the Afghan border 500km away, then maybe this is not the hotel for you. Also housing German and British embassies, it does not have the expected level of bollards and other security designed to prevent suicide bombers. Police security is very visible and there has never been a foreign terrorist attack within Turkmenistan to date.

Hotel Grand Turkmen

ul. Georogly 7. US$100 per night. Beloved by tour groups. An old Soviet hotel like the Ak Altyn. Very central, close to the Russian Bazaar and many restaurants, including the British pub. Very poor and expensive wi-fi (Charged by the hour when it is working).

Nusay Hotel

70, Galkynysh Street. US$120 per night. If you want to stay in a white marble-clad hotel in the centre of the white marble-clad government district, then this is the place for you! Modern with all the facilities expected of a 5* hotel.

Where to Eat

Ashgabat has not developed a foodie reputation, yet, but the choices are growing rapidly to include a multitude of pizza restaurants, Italian, French, US style burger bars and the British pub. Tourists are often encouraged to eat dinner at their hotels (often included in the package price). I believe hotels are great places to sleep but rarely do justice to good food at reasonable prices. This is certainly true of Ashgabat hotels. Avoid if possible.

Beware the tourist traps right next to all hotels in the city, lots of service charges appear at the end of the bill (which you would not see at restaurants geared to Turkmen) and you will pay double, or more than necessary. Take a stroll from your hotel, and go a few streets away if possible and you will find a local café, and if you can break the language barrier, you will eat well and cheaply.

Russian Bazaar (or Gulistan Market), ul. M. Kosaev. Not only packed full of fresh fruit, sides of cows, and occasional handicrafts, there are small stalls which serve shashlik and beer at the best price in Ashgabat.

British Pub, Görogly köçesi 8. Good for local beer and European and Turkish imported lagers, rather poor on British beer. Fish and Chips, Burgers and other pub fare are available. An Indian tandoori has opened alongside, it looked interesting although was closed when I was there (maybe the locals have not developed a taste for Indian food).

Altyn Cynar, Bitaral Turkmenistan St., 110. Nice BBQ restaurant, each table has a barbeque and you order thin slices of meat to cook. Expensive for what you get (you cook it yourself) but great place to socialise with a group.

Altyn Jam, Magtymgily sayoli 10. Medium to expensive restaurant specialising in Turkmen food, a large variety of lamb, beef and chicken dishes with an English menu. Some vegetarian dishes are available, but I am not sure how far I would trust them, as meat seems to get added to all dishes including the plain rice.

Travelling in Ashgabat

Taxis

In Ashgabat every one is a cabbie, except at the airport where only official taxis are allowed. Drivers like to supplement their income, and if you show the slightest inclination in needing a car (merely looking at a driver will cause them to stop) you will get a lift. TM$1 will get you almost anywhere in the city. Note that the driving standard can be poor and seatbelts are not always provided.

While driving in Ashgabat I was surprised how well mannered drivers seemed to be, always stopping well before the lights turned red at road junctions, unlike other parts of the world. It was not until my second day that I realised that at every traffic light, and there are lots of them, a policeman was standing, or hiding close to the street. There is no need for red light cameras here.

Also you will get fined if your car is dirty, which can be a big ask in a city that is afflicted with sand storms.

The reality is that the police did not need a reason to stop you. Two 'taxis' I used at night were both stopped by the police for no apparent reason. I helped the drivers out by paying the TM$5 fine. I was told by one driver that being a policeman was a very sought after job, the expectation was that you could triple your pay by collecting fines.

Buses

There are plentiful and modern buses connecting the suburbs, and wherever your hotel is, to the centre of town. Expect to pay no more than TMT$0.50 per journey. One of the more intriguing architectural sights in Ashgabat is the bus stops. Some are a completely enclosed air-conditioned oasis, whose doors open when a bus arrives, but the best ones were open to the elements with air conditioning still being pumped into them from the roof (do not forget the free electricity!) resulting in them being shrouded in a water droplet mist. This is great on a summer's day when walking past.

White marble and gold domed Presidential Palace and Parliament Buildings in Ashgabat.

Walking

This is the best way to see the city, particularly if you are staying close to the centre of the city. You will see so much more, including the huge number of bored policeman. Walk 100 meters and you are almost guaranteed to see at least two, either relaxing twirling their night sticks, or adding to their income by stopping traffic on an alleged misdemeanour.

The central part of Ashgabat is easy to walk through, and a lot of the major sites are here. Pedestrians are well catered for with wide pavements and lots of traffic light controlled crossings (do not jaywalk, you will be fined).

Things to see in Ashgabat

The Monument of Neutrality in Ashgabat

The white marbled centre of Ashgabat

After being the world's number one importer of expensive Italian marble for the last ten years, Ashgabat has finally achieved an entry in the Guinness Book of Records in 2013 for the highest density of white marble buildings in the world. The total area of marbled buildings in the city is 4,514,000 km2. Niyazov would be proud. The Presidential Palace and Parliament buildings are particularly impressive combinations of marble and gold. You can walk through here, but hide your camera, as even having it on display will lead to you being stopped by the police.

The Monument of Neutrality

Built in 1998, but moved in 2010. 3km North of the Independence monument, built to celebrate a vote to support Niyazov's personal vision of a neutral Turkmenistan, which incorporated a massive, revolving 15 metre gold statue of Niyazov on the top, which revolved to always face the sun. Even Berdimuhamedow thought that this monument may be going a bit far, and he moved it, rebuilding a smaller version of it in the suburbs. Strangely he decided to keep the statue, although sadly removed the revolving mechanism.

The Ruhnama Monument

Next to the Independence monument is the lasting monument to the Ruhnama. Niyazov's book provides theories on history, life and the universe, in all of which he played an important part. The longer he lived the more important the book became, firstly becoming a part of the driving test, then job applicants being quizzed on its contents as part of job interviews, until finally Niyazov had a word with God, and upon reading it three times you would automatically be admitted to heaven

The Ruhnama became a supporting strut to his personality cult, school children discarded their history books to read it, Imams were forced to display it next to the Quran in mosques (forced being the operative word, mosques would be demolished if the Imam did not agree), and the Russians kindly released a copy from their space shuttle, so it could also

The Ruhnama Monument in Ashgabat.

conquer space. There is even a building, the Health ministry, which has been built in the shape of the Ruhnama.

I bought one as a souvenir and expected it to be a hilarious look into the mind of an obsessive megalomaniac. Sadly, although long and somewhat dull, it stands out more as a conservative, old-fashioned self-help book, with Niyazov portraying himself as a kindly father figure with all the answers.

What is the Niyazov method of happiness? Work hard, be good to your parents, celebrate living in the best country in the world, and accept your lot. This is clearly most important, don't try and change your life (or your government) by accepting that life is predetermined by destiny. He tells an ancient Turkmen story to reinforce that point:

"An altruistic man wants to help a poor man from the village. So the rich man drops a bag full of gold onto a bridge in the way of a poor man. The poor man passes by on the bridge with closed eyes. He does not see the bag, and he hits it, pushing it into the water."

I would have a few questions of this tale, the poor man seems to lack commonsense crossing a bridge with his eyes closed (why would you do that?) and surely he would open them again if he walked into a heavy bag? But anyway, although a literary classic it is not, it does give you an understanding of his conservative views (i.e. please do not challenge me) with a healthy dose of Turkmen folk history, and a strong anti Soviet message. He clearly had not forgiven his previous paymasters.

Since his death the book has loosened its grip on life in Turkmenistan. It is still in schools, but not used for job interviews anymore. And criticising it, while maybe not wise depending on the audience, will no longer see you cast into prison for a long period of time.

The monument built by Niyazov to the Ruhnama is open everyday. At **8PM** the book opens and a ghostly recording recites a page out of the good book. These days the readings are sparsely attended in the large square, two men, their dogs (making a comeback after Niyazov banned them throughout Turkmenistan for being smelly), and the occasional tourist have the place to themselves.

Ashgabat National Museum of History

Novofiryuzinskoye Shosse. TM$35 (Camera TM$30). An absolute must see. There are several galleries devoted to Turkmenistan's long history, with some great artifacts from Merv and other desert sites, which are well worth viewing. However, it is the other galleries in the museum (actually the majority of the galleries) devoted to President Berdimuhamedow, which provide the most entertainment.

Any doubts that the President is trying to be a more modern leader, and not embarking on a personality cult like his predecessor, are blown

The Independence Monument in Ashgabat.

away as you walk around. He can only be embarking on a similar desire to be a living god with so much space and history devoted to him.

He has yet to publish his "bible", although compilations of his speeches are available in all bookshops, and his pictures are plastered on many walls (and aircraft). Yet it is this recently opened new area of the national museum devoted to the President, which kind of gives it away. I spent a happy hour wandering through three floors (yes, three floors) devoted to Berdimuhamedow. Maybe unsurprisingly I was the only person there. Unintentionally hilarious, the exhibits show shockingly photoshopped images of the President as a guitarist, accordion player (reminding me of a more rotund version of the Greek musician Yanni), motor racing driver (a cut out model of him is next to his actual winning car), swordsman, ice hockey player, sheep herder, jockey (which might have been best hidden after the recent mishap after winning his last race, see http://www.bbc.co.uk/news/world-asia-22352281) and hero in every possible way.

Outside is the 4th largest flagpole in the world. In Niyazov's time it was the largest, it may well be lengthened soon.

Independence Monument

Surrounded by parkland displaying statues of famous Turkmen from throughout history. Niyazov gets his own monument, 120 meters high, with a lift to take you to the top for a great view of central Ashgabat. Locals have nicknamed it the Toilet Plunger for some reason.

Alem Entertainment Centre

Opened in 2012 at a reported cost of US$90 million this is Turkmenistan's attempt to compete with the London Eye and the Singapore Flyer. A huge Ferris wheel dominates the entertainment park, built in the shape of an eight sided star (a motif of Oguz Khan, a legendary Turkmen warrior) measuring 47.60 metres high and with a diameter of 57 metres. It is the largest enclosed Ferris wheel in the world. Cafes and cinemas can also be found here, along with a fascinating planetarium, with a room that gives you the opportunity to feel like you are walking on the moon leaving actual footprints behind, until the next person enters. Great for Kids.

Ertugrul Gazi Mosque

Sewcenko k./Lewitan bul, Another enormous splurge by Niyazov to build a massive mosque close to the centre of Ashgabat.

The impressive minarets of Ertugrul Gazi Mosque in Ashgabat.

Modelled on the blue mosque in Istanbul, it is a thing of beauty. Even on the hottest days it is wonderfully cool and serene inside the dome. It is not popular amongst the City's Muslim faithful, due to a belief that it is cursed because of the large number of deaths of workers during the building of the Mosque.

Ashgabat TV Tower

Visible from all over Ashgabat this is another Guinness record winner. Not for its size, an impressive 211 metres, but for it being the worlds largest architectural representation of a star (another reminder of Oguz Khan).

Located 20 km from Ashgabat it offers tremendous views of the Kopet Dag mountains towards Iran, and the sprawl of Ashgabat from the viewing platform on level 30. There is also a revolving restaurant, a welcome throwback to last century when it seemed to be mandatory for all tall objects to have revolving restaurants.

Turkmenbashi Cable Car

An alternative to the TV tower is to travel into the Kopet Dag mountain range and ride a cable car close to the top.

Located 15km from Ashgabat the cable car takes you to a 1293 metre peak, which on a clear day gives you a clear view of how Ashgabat rises out of the surrounding desert. The mountains are clearly not spectacular enough, so the authorities have built an artificial waterfall next to the top, as well as the requisite cafes and a restaurant.

No public transport is available, so you should take a taxi for approx TM$10 to the cable car base. Apart from at weekends it is pretty quiet, so you may have to ask the Taxi to wait. The Cable car costs TM$2 each way.

Other Sites in Ashgabat

For more views of the Kopert Dag range, the newly built centre for weddings resembles the Burj Al Arab hotel in Dubai, coated in black marble and shaped like a sail.

The world of Turkmenbashi Tales is Ashgabats answer to Disneyworld, except with less rides, and despite opening in 2005 at acost of US$50 million is starting to look rundown.

The earthquake memorial, next to the Presidential Palace, has an interesting museum beneath it, showing the massive destruction in 1948 and the clean up efforts, with some shocking before and after photos.

Outside of Ashgabat

Nissa

Nissa, 20 km outside of Ashgabat, was the ancient capital of the Parthian Empire. **Entry at TM$25** (Camera TM$20) is quite expensive for what can actually be seen. Nissa was one of the great palaces of the region, rivalling the Assyrian cities. It was founded on an oasis at the foot of the Kopet Dag Mountains. Sadly the frequent earthquakes and the weather (mud brick can only withstand so much rain) have reduced the site to its foundations. No original substantial buildings remain, except the city wall, and there have been some attempt to rebuild the inner citadel.

Archaeological digs continue to unearth many treasures, displayed in the National museum, which you should visit first.

The Earthen city wall of Nissa with Niyazov's great walk in the hills behind.

Even in the archaeological remains of Nissa you cannot get away from ex-President Niyazov. In the photo above you can see the 20 km marble and rock running track he built in the Kopag Dag mountain range, the 'Walk of Life'.

Niyazov thought that the people in his country were unfit (he should have visited either the US or Australia to see how unfit populaces could really be), and designed a running track through the mountains. He commanded all his cabinet ministers to set an example and run the testing mountain track once a year. To add insult to injury Niyazov would start the runners off, before jumping in his personal helicopter to congratulate the winners at the finishing line. If his ministers failed to finish they were threatened with the loss of their job. Perhaps if Niyazov had joined in the run, he may not have died at such an early age.

The Gypjak Mosque.

The deserted mosque at Gypjak.

M37. Gypjak. About 15 km outside of Ashgabat is another great mosque of white Italian marble and gold. Gypjak is where Niyazov was born.

Again, it is surprisingly devoid of any worshippers (not a lot of people live in its proximity) but it is worth seeing as it is both impressive in size and design, and is the resting place of Niyazov. A smaller version of the Gypjak mosque in its grounds contains his tomb.

Altyn Asyr (Tolkucha) Market, Choganly

Do not believe older guidebooks which say that the market is 2 to 3 km from the centre of Ashgabat. It has moved, from Tolkucha to Choganly, has been rebuilt, and is now about 20km away from Ashgabat. A local taxi (Ashgabat resident with a car) will take you there for US$5, an official taxi will cost five to ten times this much. It is still the **largest open air market in Central Asia.**

Bargaining for camels at the Altyn Asyr Bazaar.

The big days are still the weekends, particularly Sundays, when buyers and sellers pour in from all over Turkmenistan and Iran. Almost everything you can imagine is for sale here. Huge amounts of fresh produce, carpets, home wares, cars, trucks, fire engines, statues, and camels are available.

The camel market is quite impressive. I quite like camels, from a distance. They add that bit of exoticism to photos if you can get them in the foreground. Up close they are a bit smelly, and prone both to spitting and sudden lurches towards you.

"What do they do with the camels they buy?" I asked my guide of the two men who were haggling over a price for a camel. A shrug of the shoulders, causing a long quizzical stare back from me, was followed by her actually asking the neatly hatted gentlemen. Did they want them for racing, food, exotic pets?? No, they were for investment. They were using them for wealth creation, converting their Manat into something tangible that they could touch, hold, and be spat on by.

You will probably be the only tourist at the busy market, and you can spend hours looking at the camels, produce, and tables of antiques that are brought in from the desert. Some of the antique arrow-heads, coins and pottery might be fake, but most seem genuine. However, none can be officially exported.

There are a huge number of carpets, mainly modern and probably coming from China. The older carpets are fewer in number, but beautiful in their states of disrepair, coming from traders in Iran as well as Turkmenistan. If you are tempted to haggle and buy one of these, remember that carpets older than thirty years cannot be exported without official inspection and certification that they are not of historical or cultural value (see the 'What to buy' section at the beginning of this guide).

One of the more popular purchases for locals was a live sheep, to be used for a wedding or birthday celebration. These were purchased for approximately US$100, had their feet tied, and were thrown in the trunk of the car. A typically Turkmen take-away food.

Lamb Kebab to go. A Takeaway from Altyn Asyr Market

Geok Depe Fortress

Located approximately 40 km west from Ashgabat are the remains of the Geok Depe fortress. The location beneath the mountains and in the oasis of Ahal is spectacular. This was the last bastion of independence against Russian control of Turkmenistan, and in fact all of Central Asia, until it fell to the Russian forces in 1881 after a 23 day siege.

It was a somewhat mismatched battle, with only 6,000 Russians trying to capture the fort held by 25,000 Turkmen troops. Under the leadership of General Mikhail Skobelev the Russians used their superior tactics, and latest technology to overcome the defenders. The siege was ended by the Russian forces digging a tunnel under the main wall and then detonating a huge mine, causing the wall to collapse and allowing the troops to pour in.

The Turkmen soldiers, and the 40,000 civilians sheltering in the complex, fled in panic, and many were massacred on the plains surrounding the fortress. Farmers still regularly come across human bones as they plough their fields in this area.

A historically important spot, only portions of the fortress wall survive. There is a small museum located next to the original gate with original weapons and ammunition.. The Gok depe mosque, the second largest in Turkmenistan, has been built close to the site to commemorate the battle.

Derweze – The Gate to Hell

The Gate of Hell at Derweze

A must-see sight while in Turkmenistan, not least because the government is now intent on removing this from tourists' itineraries by putting the flames in the burning hole in the ground out.

The 'Gate to Hell' (also sometimes called the 'Door of Hell') is close to Derweze (locally known as Darvaza, which translates to 'Gate' in Persian), in Ahal Province. It is a massive hole in the middle of a natural gas field, which has been burning since it was ignited by Soviet engineers in 1971.

It is situated in the middle of the Kara Kum desert, approximately 300 km from Ashgabat. You need to ensure you have Derweze listed on your green entry pass, as you will be stopped at police roadblocks, and they may ask to see this. If you have not got it listed, work through a local tourist agency that should be able to arrange it, at a price (see the list of Agencies at the back of this guide).

No public transport goes to Derweze. You can travel in a mini-bus from Ashgabat to Dashoguz, and ask to be dropped near the site (photographs of the crater and saying "Gaz" will help the locals understand where you want to go) and walk the 6 sandy km from the turn off (four-wheel drive access only) or wait for a lift. The crater is rarely visited, you may well be the only person there, and there are no facilities.

The easy option is to arrange a tour out of Ashgabat. Two-day tours through an agency listed in Appendix 2 will cost approximately US$250, and are worth it.

The Road Trip to the Gate to Hell.

We left Ashgabat around lunchtime in a convoy of three 4WD cars, packed with tents, sleeping bags, food, water, and, of course, many bottles of vodka.

We were heading for Derweze in the Kara Kum desert. This is the site of a Soviet mining accident in 1971 when Russian geologists were drilling for oil. They found gas instead, and the drilling rig collapsed into a crater, luckily no lives were lost. The gas was expected to burn out within days, yet 43 years later it is still burning brightly. The crater has a diameter of 70 meters (230 ft) and a depth of 25 meters (70ft).

The roads to Derweze were positively medieval. The road surface had melted in the +50 Celsius summer temperatures creating massive wheel ruts and tracks. We spent more time driving beside the road than actually on it, and the experience was similar to that of being on a continual theme park roller coaster.

The drivers drive as fast as they can, and the four-wheel drives get a full workout. We stopped a few times for toilet breaks, although not in public lavatories but in the dunes, or behind the bushes.

The 'Gate to Hell' gets a lot of geological attention, for all the right reasons. It is spectacular. But there are other intriguing geological formations that can be seen on the way

The Kara Kum Desert Sinkhole

The Kara Kum Desert Sinkhole, 10km from Derweze.

This Sinkhole is about 4 hours north of Ashgabat. It is a few minutes off the main road, on an unmarked track, with only goats for company. As with the 'Gate to Hell' there are signs of the abundant natural gas around, with flames burning at the bottom of the hole. The Sink Hole in itself would be a massive tourist attraction, if Derweze was not up the road, and if Turkmenistan became more tourist-friendly.

The Sinkhole is also blamed on the Russians, but it looks like a classic geological feature caused by weakness in the underlying rocks, with the added feature of burning gas at the bottom.

The Gate to Hell

Leaving the Sinkhole we drove for another thirty minutes, mainly off – road through the sand, arriving at about 19:30 to set up camp on sand dunes on a ridge, and look at the burning hole beneath us.

The Gate to Hell at Derwaze at dusk

As the sun went down the crater began to dominate the landscape. It had been visible before, but with darkness, and no moon, it was giving off a huge orange glow and the flames could be seen leaping out.

The drivers erected tents on the side of a hill south of the crater. This meant we had no pungent gas and sulphur smells wafting over us. Barbequed chicken, tomatoes, bread (Russian black loaves), grapes, and copious amounts of vodka were consumed as we watched the show in front of us. From 500 meters away there was no noise, and all around was silent. We watched the glowing fire of the crater against the black of the desert, while shooting stars streaked across the sky.

Gone midnight, it was time to actually go down to the crater...

The heat coming from the crater was intense. I could feel my face burning as if under hot sun. The smell, not surprisingly, was pure gas. It was like being in front of a stove with all four rings on, but not ignited.

Tourists at the edge of the Gate to Hell at Derweze

I wandered close to the edge, but not too close, as the earth was crumbling and burnt at the edges. Fall in and you would be instantly cremated. Many fires were burning in the crater, and flames leapt from spot to spot, flaring as they moved, sometimes the flares would jump to the very edge of the crater. The noise was unrelenting, a constant roaring.

I stayed there until the early hours, taking advantage of the heat. Despite 40C temperatures in daylight the thermometer dropped to low single figures at night. The tents were small, of the two-man variety, but comfortable with a thin ground mattress and sleeping bag provided.

Far Flung Tip:

Note: There are no facilities of any kind. This is the middle of the desert. Sand dunes are plentiful, and there are so few tourists you can easily find a spot to perform your ablutions, and the wind will blow sand to cover them up. Take your own toilet paper.

It was, and is, an incredible experience. But sadly it may not last much longer. The President stopped by recently and was not impressed. He saw it as waste of Turkmenistan's natural resources and ordered it put out, using helicopters to drop earth and water. Let's hope he changes his mind, as this is by far one of the most unusual tourist attractions in Turkmenistan.

Gurganj

The intricate geometric patterns in the dome of the Turabeg Khanum Mausoleum

On the Northern edge of the Kara Kum desert are the silent and impressive remains of Gurganj (also known as Urgench, or more recently as Konye-Urgench), once one of the most important cities on the Silk Road. Much of the massive city remains unexcavated, leaving an eerie landscape with only a few buildings that were spared the onslaughts of Genghis Khan and Tamerlane.

The nearest city is **Dashoguz.**

Travel

Fly: Dashoguz airport has daily flights to Ashgabat (approximate cost is US$20).

Train: Trains run twice a day to Ashgabat.

Coach and Mini Bus: Make the seven hour journey to Ashgabat from close to the Bazaar. They depart when full.

Taxi: The ancient city of Gurganj is a one hour journey (Taxi: US$30 each way) from Dashoguz.

Travel from Uzbekistan: Five years ago it was an easy day trip from Khiva, two hours across the border in Uzbekistan, but with the complex visa requirements these days, this is a lot more difficult. It is possible to conduct this as an expensive day trip (visa costs and Guide/Car for approximately US$200). A double entry Uzbekistan visa is also required. Contact Advantours in Uzbekistan see Appendix 2.

Where to Stay

Dashoguz is a modern and fairly unexciting city, but has more accommodation options than Kunya Urgench next to the ruins.

Hotel Diyarbekir, Turkmenbashi St (US$50 Room). Older style hotel, with breakfast.

Hotel Uzboy, Turkmenbashi St (US$30 Single/US$50 Double) for a modern hotel with breakfast. Pool and Wifi (extra cost).

History

Once one of the most important cities on earth, where trade and religion combined to produce a Silk Road metropolis, Gurganj was unlucky enough to be destroyed three times by invaders, resurrecting and rebuilding itself until the last destruction 800 years ago.

Khorezm was a small country sandwiched between the Persians and Uzbeks. Gurganj was its capital, located on the Oxus River. It thrived due to the money from trade, and was an important stopover, and trading centre for the camel caravans, on the northern part of the Silk Road heading to Russia and the Caspian Sea.

After being destroyed and looted by the Seljuq Turks, Gurganj and the Khorezm Empire flourished, expanding its boundaries into both Iraq and Afghanistan in the twelfth century. A Mongol historian, Juvani, described the town before the arrival of Genghis Khan as "*A dwelling place of the celebrities of mankind, its environs were receptacles for the rarities of the time, its' mansions were resplendent with every kind of lofty idea.*"

This was not to last, the country's leader, Shah Mohammed II, made a far-reaching mistake in 1219. Overestimating his country's power, he ordered the massacre of a 500-camel caravan train from the rival Mongol empire in the border town of Otrar, with all its goods, including gold and silver, confiscated. Unusually the Mongols, who respected Khorezm and thought of the country as an ally, embarked on diplomacy to rebuild the relationship, sending envoys to ask for the head of the Otrar governor as recompense. The Shah ordered one of the envoys killed, and the others to have their beards singed off. Not unsurprisingly this was the end of diplomacy, and Genghis Khan was so enraged he organised a force to descend on Khorezm.

Each Mongol soldier was tasked to slay 24 inhabitants in Gurganj, which would mean the entire population would be annihilated. Despite regularly breaking into the city, and engaging in hand to hand fighting in the small streets, the invaders failed to defeat the city. After resisting a six-month siege, the Mongols, in a clever engineering feat, diverted the Oxus to flood and drown the city's defenders.

The Silk Road would not let Gurganj die. The city was rebuilt and within one hundred years was flourishing again, only to be destroyed by another invader this time from Uzbekistan. Tamerlane (Timur) invaded, mainly because he considered the city a dangerous economic rival to his prosperous city of Samarkand. In 1388 he destroyed much of the city, sowing barley over its remains and forcing many of the population to move to Samarkand.

Today the whole area is devoid of life except for a few buildings that were spared, or rebuilt from the invading armies' destruction.

Things to see:

Turabeg Khanum Mausoleum

The partially ruined Turabeg Khanum Mausoleum was built in 1370. The outer dome has partially collapsed, and the inner dome is leaking badly, but it is more impressive for its authenticity and lack of restoration. Over the border in Uzbekistan the Mausoleum would have been completely rebuilt and lost much of its charm.

The partially ruined Turabeg Khanum Mausoleum

The outer dome, once one of the largest in Central Asia, has been destroyed, but the beautiful inner dome has mostly survived and has exquisite mosaic geometric patterns, with 365 stars representing the night sky, and calendar year

Kutlug Timur Minaret

The largest building left standing from the destruction was the minaret of Kutlug Timur. Built between 1320 to 1330, and over 200 feet

The huge minaret at Kutlug Temir in Gurganj.

high (62 meters), it was the tallest building on earth in the 14th century.

Tamerlane was so in awe of its size when his forces arrived to destroy the city, he ordered it to be spared.

The diameter at the base is 12 metres, and at the top 2 metres. It has eighteen patterned stripes surrounding it with three of them having inscriptions in Kufic (pre Islamic Arabic).

Today, having survived invasions and earthquakes, it has become one of the most holy sites in Turkmenistan. Pilgrims come from all over the country to walk counter clockwise around the minaret three times while saying their prayers. Foreigners come and struggle to fit the whole minaret into their viewfinders.

Sultan Tekeş Mausoleum

The only building to be rebuilt is the Soltan Tekeş Mausoleum, a short walk from the minaret. The beautiful blue dome makes up for the modern brickwork. The Sultan was the 12th century leader who expanded the Khorezm empire into Afghanistan. He built this mausoleum for himself before he died to impress the living of his greatness, along with a Madrassah and a library, neither of which have been rebuilt. Originally the Mausoleum stood thirty metres high and rivaled the Sultan Sanjar Mausoleum in its size and beauty.

Beyond this is the base of an earlier Mamun II minaret, began in 1011, but never finished beyond its stump.

Forty Mullahs Hill

This where the inhabitants of Gurganj fought their final and bloody stand against the Mongols. Although not much to look at from a distance, the mound of rubble and mud is being excavated, revealing the remains of walls, pottery and human remains. If you look carefully you may see the odd human bone sticking out of the mud. Archaeological digs are becoming more frequent at this recently proclaimed UNESCO site, and there is much more to uncover.

Il-Arslan Mausoleum

Behind the Kutlug Timur minaret is the Il-Arslan Mausoleum. It has a distinctive conical dome, and is one of the oldest surviving buildings in Gurganji.

The dome is an unusual twelve-sided pyramid on top of a square building. The decorative brickwork has only survived near the top of the Mausoleum, but it gives you a good idea how imposing it would have looked upon completion.

Nejameddin Kubra and Sultan Ali Mausoleums

Ten minutes walk North from the Kutlug Timur minaret detouring through the modern city are the Nejameddin Kubra and Sultan Ali Mausoleums. Tourists often miss these as they are a little way away from the main site, but they are well worth a visit.

The Mausoleums face each other across a large courtyard. From a distance they look identical, but up close it can be seen that the Nejameddin Kubra Mausoleum has a much larger dome. It is also the more decorative, being covered with many tiles with original Islamic writing.

Nejameddin Kubra was a famous 12th- and 13th-century Khorezm Muslim teacher and poet, who founded the Dervish order of Kubraviya, and is widely revered today. It is a major site for pilgrimage with many pilgrims visiting and prostrating themselves, even of a weekday

The Mausoleum was built in the 14th century and is made up of four domes. Originally an obelisk marked the spot where the Kubra was beheaded by the Mongols during their invasion. This was destroyed when the dome fell down in the 1970's and has yet to be restored.

The Sultan Ali Mausoleum is less ornate, due to never being fully completed. It was built for the ruler of Gurganj in the 16th Century, but due to the successful invasion by the Bukhara Khan it was abandoned.

Links:

Turkmenistan Consul in US: http://turkmenistanembassy.org/

Turkmenistan Consul in UK: http://turkmenembassy.org.uk/

CIA Guide to Turkmenistan:
https://www.cia.gov/library/publications/the-world-factbook/geos/tx.html

Weather in Ashgabat:
http://www.weatherbase.com/weather/weather.php3?s=8883

Lonely Planet: http://www.lonelyplanet.com/turkmenistan

A Study on Personality Cults: http://www.vocativ.com/01-2014/inside-turkmenistans-presidential-personality-cults/

Paul Theroux, a Letter from Turkmenistan:
http://www.newyorker.com/reporting/2007/05/28/070528fa_fact_theroux

Recommended Reading

Paul Theroux – Ghost Train to the Eastern Star. *(Penguin, 2009)* A chapter on Turkmenistan which is full of Theroux's witty commentary, train travel, Ashgabat, Merv, and a run-in with the secret police.

Calum Macleod-Bradley Mayhew. – Uzbekistan. The golden road to Samarkand. *(Odyssey Books and Guides, 2011)* Primarily an excellent tour guide to Uzbekistan, but does provide information on the border towns, particularly Kunya Urgench, and context to the recent political upheavals in the Central Asia

Paul Brummel –Turkmenistan the Travel Guide *(Bradt Travel Guides.2006).* Written by an ex diplomat living in the country. Great context and political stories, although a little outdated. Expensive, even second-hand, possibly because there are so few guides to Turkmenistan

Ahmed Rashid – Jihad. The Ride of Militant Islam in Central Asia. *(Penguin, 2002)* Interesting political and economic analysis of the key Central Asian nations, including Turkmenistan, and the future potential risks of being located next to a stronger and unpredictable Afghanistan. Written over ten years ago, but still relevant.

Justin Marozzi – Tamerlane, Sword of Islam Conqueror of the World. *(Harper Perennial, 2005)* A good history of Tamerlane, who is still little known in the Western world. Sympathetic, although Tamerlane's extreme methods of subjugating opponents might surprise even Genghis Khan. Best when Marozzi stays on subject, he has a tendency to wander off topic at times.

Appendix I: Turkmenistan Embassies and Consulates.

Austria

Vienna, Argentinierstrasse 22/2, StiegeII / EG. Tel.: 810-431503647023
email: turkmenistan.botschaft@chello.at

Azerbaijan

AZ1078, Baku, street Mammedguluzade Jalil, 85/266. Tel. :810-994125963527

email: turkmen.embaz@gmail.com

Belgium

Brussels, Boulevard General Jacques street, 15, 1050. Tel. :810-3226481874

email: turkmenistan@skynet.be

China

Beijing, 100016, street Xiaoyunlu, 18, King's Garden Villas. Tel.: 810-861065326975

email: embturkmen@netchina.com.cn

France

Paris, 13 rue Picot 75116. Tel.: 810-33153651071

email: turkmenamb@orange.fr

Germany

Berlin, Botschaft von Turkmenistan Langobardenallee 14 14052.

Tel. :810-493030102451

email: info@botschaft-turkmenistan

India

New-Delhi, C-11, West end Colony. Tel. :810-919910999515

email: turkmen@airtelmail.int or tkmemb@airtelmail.in

Iran

Teheran, street Vatanpur Barati, 34. Tel.: 810-982122206731

email: info@botschaft-turmenisatn.de

Japan

Tokio, Shibuya-ku, Higashi 2-6-14. Tel.:81-3-5766-1150

email: turkmenistan.jp@gmail.com

Kazahkstan

Astana,Otyrarskaya street, 8/1. Tel. :810-7172211199

email: tmemb@astanatelekom.kz

Malaysia

Kuala-Lumpur, 14/346, Wisma Sin Heap Lee, Jalan Tun Razak, 50400
Tel.:+60321610421; +60321610490

email: tkmembmalaysia@gmail.com

Russian Federation

Moscow, Filippovskiy passage, 22. Tel. :810-74956916636

email: turkmen@dol.ru

Switzerland

Geneva, Avenue de France, 1202. Tel. :810-41227491005

Tajikistan

Dushanbe, street Ahu-Babaev, 10. Tel.: 810 - (992) 2242640
email: turkmenemtj@gmail.com

Turkey

Ankara, street KozaSokak, 28, Chankaya. Tel. :810-903124417123

email: tmankara@ttnet.net.tr

United Kingdom

131 Holland Park Avenue, London. W11 4UT. Tel. :810-442072551071

email: www.turkmenembassy.org.uk

United States of America

Washington, DC: 2207, Massachusetts Ave., NW 20008. Tel. :810-1 (202)
5881500

email: turkmen@mindspring.com

Uzbekistan

Tashkent, Mirobad region, street Afrasiab, 19.

Tel. :810-99871256-94-02

email: trkmemb@mail.ru

Appendix II: Travel agents authorised to process Letters of Introduction (LOIs) in Turkmenistan.

Dag Syyahat
Azadi street, 69, hotel "Dayhan" Ashgabat, Turkmenistan, 744000
Tel: +(99312) 93 16 43, 93 25 59
e-mail: dag_syyahat@online.tm; tss@online.tm
website: www.dagtravel.net

Owadan Tourism
65 Azady Street, Ashgabat, Turkmenistan, 744000
Tel/Fax: +993 12 930486
email: trowadan@online.tm
website: www.owadan.net

Ayan Travel
Tel.: 35-29-14, 35-07-97
e-mail: ayan@online.tm
website: www.ayan-travel.com

Elkhan-Syyakhat
Tel/Fax: 39-84-07, 35-71-28
e-mail: elkhantour@online.tm

Ahalsyyahat
Tel.: 35-05-90, 27-37-67
e-mail: infoahaltravel@gmail.com

DN Tours
Tel.: 27-04-49, 27-04-38
e-mail: admin@dntours.com, dntours@online.tm
website: www.dntours.com

Latif Travel Agency
Tel: 39-28-08; 39-29-31
e-mail: latif@online.tm
website: www.turkmenistan-latif.com

Saada
Tel/Fax: 35-20-04; 35-06-44
e-mail: saada@online.tm
website: http://www.saada-tour.com

Zehin Travel Company
Tel.: 27-46-48, Fax: 27-41-49
e-mail: zehin@online.tm

Uzbekistan:

And a very helpful agency in Tashkent, if you are travelling there before applying to go to Turkmenistan is:

Advantour Uzbekistan
Mirobod kochasi-1, 47A
Tashkent 100015
Uzbekistan
Tel: +998 71 1503020
Fax: +998 71 1503021

e-mail: tashkent@advantour.com (ask for Shavkat)

About the Author

Simon has a travel addiction, loves history, active volcanoes, punk music and local food, craft and home brewed beer. A bottle of wine and fresh bread & cheese on a beach is luxury travel.

He lives in Sydney, Australia, with an eleven year old son addicted to travelling first class (after once getting upgraded on a flight in Peru) and an adventurous wife who enjoys kayaking around Greek islands and getting close to whales in Tonga.

No pets, but various wildlife roams through his garden, from blue tongued lizards to ring tailed possums and bandicoots.

Updates on his latest travels can be found at www.farflungplaces.net and he can be contacted at simon@farflungplaces.net

Simon is also the Co-Founder of collaborative sharing exchange website: Skillstay.com. This was developed with his wife, Lea, and they built it because they had a need for a site that allowed people to travel the world for free, using only their skills as payment. The site links hosts and helpers together for an exchange of work for a room to stay in.

SkillStay.com

They love to travel and hate housework and love to share with other travelers. They encourage growing, learning and sharing.

Thank you for reading, please share your comments on Amazon and GoodReads.

A Taste of Far Flung Places on the net

Black Magic, and why Missionaries stood no chance. Ambrym. Vanuatu

Ambrym island in Vanuatu is still relatively untouched by western thoughts and values, and traditional custom beliefs remain very strong, particularly in the North East and North West villages, maybe not coincidentally the furthest settlements from the two small airports here.

The Volcano Mt Benbow is the focus for much of the beliefs (and also for the surrounding islands like Malakula and Epi, where its glowing orange lava lakes can be seen eerily in the night sky). It is dangerous, destroying a village in 1913, and its eruptions have caused evacuations on several occasions, yet it provides life through rich farming soil. Certain clans or groups are believed to be custodians of the volcano, and use it to their benefit to threaten to cause it to erupt unless they get their way in village disagreements. Conversely, when it does erupt unexpectedly they get blamed and can be forced to escape to other islands for their safety.

Certain parts of the volcano are reserved for their spirits after they die, each village has their special area. Not knowing this, the early Christian missionaries who visited the island failed dismally in their attempt to convert the local populace, the threat of a fiery end for their souls if they did not convert was not going to provoke fear when they believed that was their destiny anyway.

My guide, from North Ambrym, was a firm believer in the traditional custom ways. The lava bombs he eagerly collected that had landed overnight, close to our flimsy tents, could be buried around his land to provide protection against those families who control the eruptions of the volcano. They could also be carved into faces and placed in other people's homes to control them and cause "problems". These exact problems were not specified, but I could guess.

He was also an expert in sand drawings, a beautiful and unique way of telling ancient stories and beliefs by tracing a finger through the ash to produce intricate artwork, in an amazingly quick time. These are given as gifts to people; he kindly gave me a few drawings after I gave him my solar torch (he really needed it a lot more than I did).

This beautiful drawing is called 'The Leaf Man' and it represents the story of a local villager who went exploring and was about to be attacked by a group from a rival village. He placed a leaf on his head, and vegetation on his body for camouflage, and was able to move through the villagers without being seen. It took about thirty seconds to draw the symmetric and complex patterns, and after viewing it (and letting me quickly take one photograph) he destroyed it so others could not see it.

www.farflungplaces.net

Skillstay: Stay all over the World for Free

Skillstay is a global community that connects hosts and helpers.

Become a **HELPER** and swap your skills for a **FREE** place to stay anywhere in the world. Become a **HOST** and get the **FREE** help you need in exchange for your spare room or couch.

Locally, Nationally, Globally.

How does Skillstay work?

Helpers volunteer their specialist skills for a few hours a day in exchange for a place to stay.

Hosts get the help they need in their home or business and free up their time.

Current Skillstays include: Painting, housework, childcare, horse riding, eco-projects, farming, cooking, language lessons, website development, cattle mustering, cooking and many more.

Use only Skills as Payment. No money changes hands.

www.skillstay.com **Exchange your skills. Make new friends**

Made in the USA
Middletown, DE
08 September 2015